80 THAI CURRIES

AND CLASSIC SOUTH-EAST ASIAN RECIPES

30 THAI CURRIES
AND CLASSIC SOUTH-EAST ASIAN RECIPES

WITH REDUCED FAT FOR HEALTH AND FITNESS

The best traditional dishes of Thailand, Burma, Indonesia, Malaysia and the Philippines – authentic recipes shown in over 360 mouthwatering photographs

Jane Bamforth

southwater

This edition is published by Southwater, an imprint of Anness Publishing Ltd,
Hermes House, 88–89 Blackfriars Road, London SE1 8HA; tel. 020 7401 2077; fax 020 7633 9499
www.southwaterbooks.com; www.annesspublishing.com

If you like the images in this book and would like to investigate using them for publishing, promotions or
advertising, please visit our website www.practicalpictures.com for more information.

UK agent: The Manning Partnership Ltd;
tel. 01225 478444; fax 01225 478440; sales@manning-partnership.co.uk
UK distributor: Grantham Book Services Ltd;
tel. 01476 541080; fax 01476 541061; orders@gbs.tbs-ltd.co.uk
North American agent/distributor: National Book Network;
tel. 301 459 3366; fax 301 429 5746; www.nbnbooks.com
Australian agent/distributor: Pan Macmillan Australia;
tel. 1300 135 113; fax 1300 135 103; customer.service@macmillan.com.au
New Zealand agent/distributor: David Bateman Ltd; tel. (09) 415 7664; fax (09) 415 8892

Publisher: Joanna Lorenz
Senior Managing Editor: Conor Kilgallon
Editors: Joy Wotton and Elizabeth Woodland
Recipes: Judy Bastyra, Jane Bamforth, Mridula Baljekar, Jenni Fleetwood, Yasuko Fukuoka,
Christine Ingram, Becky Johnson, Kathy Man, Sallie Morris, Kate Whiteman
Home Economists: Annabel Ford, Becky Johnson, Lucy McKelvie, Bridget Sargeson, Helen Trent
Photographers: Martin Brigdale, Nicky Dowey, Janine Hosegood, Becky Johnson, Dave King,
William Lingwood, Craig Robertson
Designer: Nigel Partridge
Production Controller: Mai-Ling Collyer

© Anness Publishing Ltd 2007

Previously published as part of a larger volume, *Low-Fat, No-Fat Thai*

Ethical Trading Policy

At Anness Publishing we believe that business should be conducted in an ethical and ecologically
sustainable way, with respect for the environment and a proper regard to the replacement of the natural
resources we employ.

As a publisher, we use a lot of wood pulp to make high-quality paper for printing, and that wood
commonly comes from spruce trees. We are therefore currently growing more than 500,000 trees in
two Scottish forest plantations near Aberdeen – Berrymoss (130 hectares/320 acres) and West Touxhill
(125 hectares/305 acres). The forests we manage contain twice the number of trees employed each year in
paper-making for our books.

Because of this ongoing ecological investment programme, you, as our customer, can have the pleasure
and reassurance of knowing that a tree is being cultivated on your behalf to naturally replace the materials
used to make the book you are holding.

Our forestry programme is run in accordance with the UK Woodland Assurance Scheme (UKWAS) and
will be certified by the internationally recognized Forest Stewardship Council (FSC). The FSC is a non-
government organization dedicated to promoting responsible management of the world's forests.
Certification ensures forests are managed in an environmentally sustainable and socially responsible way.
For further information about this scheme, go to www.annesspublishing.com/trees

Notes

Bracketed terms are intended for American readers.
For all recipes, quantities are given in both metric and imperial measures and, where appropriate, in standard
cups and spoons. Follow one set, but not a mixture, because they are not interchangeable.
Standard spoon and cup measures are level. 1 tsp = 5ml, 1 tbsp = 15ml, 1 cup = 250ml/8fl oz.
Australian standard tablespoons are 20ml. Australian readers should use 3 tsp in place of 1 tbsp for
measuring small quantities of gelatine, flour, salt, etc.
American pints are 16fl oz/2 cups. American readers should use 20fl oz/2.5 cups in place of 1 pint
when measuring liquids.
Electric oven temperatures in this book are for conventional ovens. When using a fan oven, the temperature
will probably need to be reduced by about 10–20°C/20–40°F. Since ovens vary, you should check with your
manufacturer's instruction book for guidance.
The nutritional analysis given for each recipe is calculated per portion (i.e. serving or item), unless otherwise
stated. If the recipe gives a range, such as Serves 4–6, then the nutritional analysis will be for the smaller
portion size, i.e. 6 servings. Measurements for sodium do not include salt added to taste.
Medium (US large) eggs are used unless otherwise stated.

Each recipe title is followed by a symbol that indicates the following:

★ = 5g of fat or less per serving   ★★ = 10g of fat or less per serving

Main front cover image shows Curried Rice Vermicelli – for recipe see page 93

CONTENTS

INTRODUCTION

People living in Thailand and South-east Asia have a well-balanced diet, which is low in fat and high in fibre. The cuisines of these regions offer us a range of tasty dishes which are not only quick and easy to prepare but healthy too.

A healthy diet provides us with all the nutrients we need. By eating the right types, balance and proportions of foods, we are likely to have more energy and a higher resistance to diseases and illnesses such as heart disease, cancers, bowel disorders and obesity.

Of the five main food groups, it is recommended that we eat at least five portions of fruit and vegetables a day, not including potatoes; carbohydrate foods such as noodles, cereals, rice and potatoes; moderate amounts of fish, poultry and dairy products; and small amounts of foods containing fat or sugar. A dish like Thai Fried Rice (see page 87 for recipe) fits the prescription perfectly, with its balance of rice, chicken fillets, (bell) peppers and corn.

THE ROLE OF FAT IN THE DIET

Fats shouldn't be cut out of our diets completely; they are a valuable source of energy and make foods more palatable. Aim to limit your daily intake of fats to no more than 30–35 per cent of the total

Below: Asian cooks use a wonderful assortment of shellfish, such as mussels, from the sea, lakes, rivers and canals.

Above: Rice noodles and rice vermicelli form an integral part of the Thai and South-east Asian cuisine. Easily reconstituted, they are virtually fat free.

number of calories you consume. Each gram of fat provides nine calories, so a person eating 2,000 calories a day should not eat more than 70g/2¾oz of fat. Saturated fat should not comprise more than 10 per cent of the total calorie intake.

TYPES OF FAT

All fats in our foods are made up of building blocks of fatty acids and glycerol, and their properties vary according to each combination. The two main types of fat are saturated and unsaturated.

SATURATED FATS

The main sources of saturated fats are animal products, such as fatty cuts of meat and meat products; spreading fats that are solid at room temperature, such as butter, lard and margarine; and full-fat dairy products such as cream and cheese. Aside from meat, these ingredients are seldom found in Thai and South-east Asian recipes, but it is also important to avoid coconut and palm oil, which are saturated fats of vegetable origin.

Saturated fats are also found in many processed foods, such as chips (French fries) and savoury snacks, as well as cookies, pastries and cakes.

Above: Naturally low in fat, such fresh green vegetables as these snake or yard-long beans form a healthy part of the Thai diet.

POLYUNSATURATED FATS

There are two types: those of vegetable or plant origin, known as Omega-6, which are found in sunflower oil, soft margarine, nuts and seeds; and Omega-3 fatty acids, which come from oily fish such as tuna, salmon, herring, mackerel and sardines as well as walnuts, soya beans and wheatgerm.

THE LOW-FAT RECIPES

Each dish featured in this book includes a nutritional breakdown, providing an at-a-glance guide to calorie and fat content, as well as other key components such as protein, carbohydrate and fibre, calcium, cholesterol and sodium. Many of the recipes contain less than five grams of total fat per serving, and a few are even lower in fat. For ease of reference, all the recipes with a single ★ after the recipe title contain a maximum of five grams of total fat per portion and those with ★★ contain a maximum of 10 grams of total fat per portion.

Although these easy to cook recipes are low in fat, they lose nothing in flavour. This practical cookbook will enable you to enjoy delicious curries and other classic South-east Asian dishes with a clear conscience.

PRINCIPLES OF THAI COOKING

Food takes centre stage in the daily life of most people in Thailand and South-east Asia. Food is one of life's greatest pleasures, and sharing it with family and friends is fundamental to the cultures of these countries.

Dishes are easy to cook, with enough visual appeal to tempt anyone. Until fairly recently, recipes were not written down, but were handed down from generation to generation. The lack of written recipes has encouraged cooks to use their imagination when creating dishes, to experiment with flavours, while keeping to the principles of their local cooking styles and techniques.

Besides offering fabulous flavours, South-east Asian cooking is extremely healthy. The food is fresh, and a wide range of meats, seafood, vegetables and salads are consumed. Meat and fish are typically served in small quantities, surrounded by side dishes, flavoured with fresh herbs and other seasonings.

SPICES AND AROMATICS

South-east Asian cooks are skilled in the art of combining spices, which they use to add taste, colour and aroma.

The essential spices of South-east Asia are coriander, cumin, turmeric, chilli and peppercorns, and although the same spices are used in India, the curries of South-east Asia are quite different, with a milder heat and more subtle flavours.

South-east Asian cuisine also makes use of whole spices, which are removed at the end of cooking. These include cinnamon, cloves and cardamom pods; they are especially popular in Malaysia, where the influence of Indian cuisine is most strongly felt.

ADDING FLAVOUR

Spice blends are usually combined with coconut milk, lemon grass and kaffir lime leaves. Using reduced-fat coconut milk keeps the fat content of dishes to a minimum. Many South-east Asian curries have a distinctive tangy taste, which comes from tamarind, the souring agent that is characteristic of all Asian cooking. Lime juice and vinegar arc often used as well, adding a refreshing tartness to curries, while the addition of soy sauce, fish sauce or shrimp paste gives the particular depth and pungent flavour that is so distinctive to South-east Asian cuisine.

Among the fresh ingredients used as flavouring agents are shallots, galangal, ginger, garlic and chilli, as well as an array of fresh herbs, especially coriander (cilantro), mint and basil.

Below: Each country in South-east Asia has its own individual cooking style, but the essential approach to eating is the same: food is always fresh, full of flavour using a variety of herbs and spices, and carefully prepared and presented.

PREPARING A THAI CURRY

Despite the many regional variations, Thai and South-east Asian curries are prepared following a similar pattern. The differences in the cuisines can be attributed more to culture, lifestyle and local food resources, than to alternative cooking techniques.

BASIC INGREDIENTS

The first point to consider when making any curry is what cooking medium to use. Coconut and palm oil are widely used throughout South-east Asia, and people use lard in some countries, including Thailand and the Philippines. To avoid consuming too much saturated fat, use a lighter cooking oil instead, such as vegetable oil or sunflower oil.

In South-east Asia, stock is more frequently used than water when making curries. Stock adds an extra depth of flavour, and since many dishes use meat and poultry cooked off the bone, the ingredients are probably already to hand.

For thickening sauces, the common practice is to rely on ingredients such as reduced-fat coconut milk, grated

Below: Spices and aromatics can be used in many ways.

coconut, onions, grated fresh root ginger and crushed garlic. In all curries, colour and pungency are created by the addition of different types of chillies, in varying amounts.

COOKING A CURRY

The starting point when making a curry is to preheat the oil and fry the onions, which, along with garlic and ginger, are the basic ingredients of all Thai and South-east Asian curries. Sometimes the onions are fried until they are crisp before the garlic and ginger are added, while in other dishes they are simply softened. The spices, flavourings or pastes are then added and cooked for a short time to eliminate their raw flavour. When the spices are cooked to the right point, the oil begins to separate forming a thick, spicy curry paste.

By using a wide range of cooking techniques, a variety of flavours can be created from the same basic ingredients. Although a recipe should initially be used as a guide, it is much more fun to be able to stamp your own personality on to whatever you are cooking. This becomes easier with practice, and, after a while, using spices to prepare delicious curries

becomes a work of art. Start to use spices as an artist uses a palette, as you tone and colour the food to your own taste.

PLANNING AND SERVING

Dishes are not categorized into separate courses, but are all brought to the table at the same time. Diners help themselves with many helpings of small quantities.

Rice is the cornerstone of all meals, and is served with one or two vegetable side dishes, relishes, salads and curries. It is customary to serve more than one meat or poultry dish, a vegetable curry and a dry, spiced, stir-fried vegetable dish. A soup is another important part of the meal. Desserts are not generally served, but delicious fresh fruit is usually on offer, as well as hot and cold fruits cooked in coconut milk, sweetened with palm sugar.

FREEZING FOODS

Thai and South-east Asian curries can be cooked very quickly, as meat and vegetables are cut into small pieces in preparation for stir-frying, and they are not marinated before cooking. As time-saving strategies, therefore, chilling and freezing are probably not as important in Thai cuisine as they are to some other types of cooking. However, curries always taste better if they are cooked a day or two in advance. The spices seem to permeate the meat and poultry, and the final flavour is much more mellow. If you plan to freeze the food you are cooking, the following basic guidelines may be helpful:
• Leave the food slightly underdone.
• Cool the food rapidly. The best way to do this is to tip it into a large tray (a large roasting pan is ideal) and leave it in a cool place.
• Once the food has cooled down, put it into appropriate containers, then label and chill it before finally putting it in the freezer. The food will keep in the freezer for 6–8 months, depending on the star rating of your freezer.

Food from unplanned freezing, such as leftovers, should not be frozen for longer than 2–3 months.

FAT-FREE COOKING METHODS

Thai and South-east Asian cooking uses a variety of low-fat and fat-free cooking methods, and by incorporating recipes from this region into your daily diet it is easy to bring down your total fat consumption. Where possible, steam, microwave or grill (broil) foods, without adding extra fat. Alternatively, braise in a defatted stock, wine or fruit juice, or stir-fry with just a spray of vegetable oil.

• By choosing a good quality, non-stick wok, such as the one above, you can keep the amount of fat needed for cooking foods to the absolute minimum. When cooking meat in a regular pan, dry-fry the meat to brown it, then tip it into a sieve (strainer) and drain off the excess fat before returning it to the pan and adding the other ingredients. If you do need a little fat for cooking, choose an oil high in unsaturates, such as sunflower or corn oil and use a spray where possible.

• Eat less meat and more vegetables and noodles or other forms of pasta. A good method for making a small amount of meat such as beef steak go a long way is to place it in the freezer for 30 minutes and then slice it very thinly with a sharp knife. Meat prepared this way will cook very quickly with very little fat.

• When baking chicken or fish, wrap it in a loose package of foil or baking parchment, with a little wine or fruit juice. Add some fresh herbs or spices before sealing the parcel, if you like.

• It is often unnecessary to add fat when grilling (broiling) food. If the food shows signs of drying, lightly brush or spray it with a little unsaturated oil, such as sunflower, corn or olive oil. Microwaved foods seldom need the addition of fat, so add herbs or spices for extra flavour and colour.

• Steaming is the ideal way of cooking fish. If you like, arrange the fish on a bed of aromatic flavourings such as lemon or lime slices and sprigs of herbs. Alternatively, place finely shredded vegetables or seaweed in the base of the steamer to give the fish extra flavour.

• If you do not own a steamer, cook vegetables in a covered pan over low heat with just a little water, so that they cook in their own juices.
• Vegetables can be braised in the oven in low-fat or fat-free stock, wine or a little water with some chopped fresh or dried herbs.
• Try poaching foods such as chicken, fish or fruit in low-fat or fat-free stock or fruit juice.
• Plain rice or noodles make a very good low-fat accompaniment to most Thai and South-east Asian dishes.

• The classic Asian technique of adding moisture and flavour to chicken by marinating it in a mixture of soy sauce and rice wine, with a little sesame oil, can be used with other meats too. You can also use a mixture of alcohol, herbs and spices, or vinegar or fruit juice. The marinade will also help to tenderize the meat and any remaining marinade can be used to baste the food while it is cooking.
• When serving vegetables, resist the temptation to add butter. Instead, sprinkle with chopped fresh herbs.

Low-fat spreads in cooking
A huge variety of low-fat and reduced-fat spreads is available in supermarkets, along with some spreads that are very low in fat. Generally speaking, any very low-fat spreads with a fat content of around 20 per cent or less have a high water content. These are unsuitable for cooking and can only be used for spreading.

VEGETABLES

Naturally low in fat and bursting with vitamins and minerals, vegetables are one food group that should ideally make up the bulk of our daily diet. In Thailand and South-east Asia cooks use vegetables freely in curries and stir-fried dishes, and have evolved a wide range of delicious vegetarian main courses to make the most of the abundant choice of vegetables on sale in markets.

Many of these vegetables are now commonplace in other parts of the world. Chinese leaves (Chinese cabbage), pak choi (bok choy) and beansprouts are usually available in supermarkets, and other greens, such as mizuna, Chinese mustard greens and Chinese broccoli, are often grown by small producers and can be found at farmers' markets.

CHINESE LEAVES

Also known as Chinese cabbage or Napa cabbage, this vegetable has pale green, crinkly leaves with long, wide, white ribs. It is pleasantly crunchy, has a sweet, nutty flavour and tastes wonderful raw or cooked. When buying Chinese leaves, look out for firm, slightly heavy heads with pale green leaves without blemishes or bruises. To prepare, peel off the outer leaves, cut off the root and slice the cabbage thinly or thickly. When stir-fried, Chinese leaves lose their subtle cabbage taste and take on the flavour of other ingredients in the dish.

Below: Chinese leaves have a mild, delicate flavour.

Right: Pak choi tastes similar to spinach.

PAK CHOI

Another member of the brassica family, pak choi (bok choy) has lots of noms-de-plume, including horse's ear, Chinese cabbage and Chinese white cabbage. There are several varieties, and one or other is usually on sale at the supermarket. Unlike Chinese leaves, pak choi doesn't keep well, so plan to use it within a day or two of purchase. The vegetable is generally cooked, although very young and tender pak choi can be eaten raw. The stems – regarded by many as the best part – need slightly longer cooking than the leaves.

CHOI SUM

Often sold in bunches, choi sum is a brassica with bright green leaves and thin, pale, slightly grooved stems. It has a pleasant aroma and mild taste, and remains crisp and tender if properly cooked. The leaves can be sliced, but are more often steamed whole. Choi sum will keep for a few days in the salad drawer, but is best used as soon as possible after purchase.

CHINESE BROCCOLI

With its somewhat straggly appearance, this brassica looks more like purple sprouting broccoli than prim Calabrese. Every part of Chinese broccoli is edible, and each has its own inimitable taste. To prepare, remove the tough outer leaves, then cut off the leaves. If the stems are tough, peel them. It is usual to blanch the vegetable briefly in salted boiling water or stock before stir-frying.

AUBERGINES

Popular throughout Thailand and South-east Asia, aubergines (eggplants) come in a variety of shapes, sizes and colours. They have a smoky, slightly bitter taste and spongy flesh that readily absorbs other flavours and oils. To avoid the absorption of too much fat, cut the aubergine into slices, and dry-fry these in a wok over medium heat for 4–5 minutes. They can also be braised, stuffed or baked.

MOOLI

Also known as daikon, this Asian vegetable looks rather like a parsnip, but is actually related to the radish. The flavour is milder than that of most radishes, however, although the texture is similar: crisp and crunchy. Treat it like a carrot, scraping or peeling the outer skin and then slicing it in rounds or batons. It can be eaten raw or cooked.

BAMBOO SHOOTS

Fresh bamboo shoots are quite hard to buy outside Asia, but you may find them in big-city Asian markets. They must be parboiled before being cooked, as the raw vegetable contains a highly toxic oil. Remove the base and the hard outer leaves, then cut the core into chunks. Boil these in salted water for 30 minutes, then drain, rinse under cold water and drain again. Cut into slices, shreds or cubes for further cooking. Dried bamboo slices must be soaked in water for 2–3 hours before use. Canned bamboo shoots only need rinsing before being used.

Below: Choi sum is often used in stir-fries.

Above: Thai cooking uses green apple aubergines and purple long aubergines.

WATER CHESTNUTS

Fresh, crisp water chestnuts are the corms of a plant that grows on the margins of rivers and lakes. Their snow-white flesh stays crunchy even after long cooking. Fresh water chestnuts are often available from Asian markets. They keep well in a paper bag in the refrigerator. Once released from their dark brown jackets, they must be kept submerged in water in a covered container and used within one week. Canned water chestnuts should be rinsed before being used.

Below: Mooli has a crisp, crunchy texture and is delicious raw.

BEANSPROUTS

Mung beans and soy beans are the varieties of beansprout most often used, and they are an important ingredient in the Asian kitchen. It is important to use them as fresh as possible. Better still, sprout the beans yourself. Before use, rinse them to remove the husks and tiny roots. Use them in salads or stir-fries, but take care not to overcook them, or they will become limp and tasteless.

SPRING ONIONS

Slender and crisp, spring onions (scallions) are appreciated by Asian cooks not only for their aroma and flavour, but also for their perceived cooling qualities. Use spring onions raw in salads or lightly cooked in stir-fries. They need very little preparation. Just trim off the roots, strip off the wilted outer leaves and separate the white and green parts. Spring onion green is sometimes used in Asian dishes as ribbon, to tie tiny parcels of food, in which case it is first blanched so that it becomes more flexible.

MUSHROOMS

Several types of mushrooms are used in Asian cooking, and many of these are now available in Western supermarkets.

Shiitake mushrooms are prized in Asia, both for their flavour and their medicinal qualities. They have a slightly acidic taste and a meaty, slippery texture. They contain twice as much protein as button mushrooms and their robust flavour makes them the ideal partner for noodles and rice.

To prepare fresh shiitake mushrooms, remove the stems. The caps can be left whole, or sliced. If they are to be used in a salad, cook them briefly in low-fat stock first.

Dried shiitake mushrooms must be reconstituted before being used. Soak them in cold water overnight, or in a bowl of warm water for at least 30 minutes before using, then strain the soaking liquid. Remove the stems before use.

Right: Spring onions are used raw in salads.

Oyster mushrooms have a mild flavour and are pastel-coloured in shades of pink, yellow or pearl grey. They need gentle handling. Tear, rather than cut, large specimens and don't overcook them, or they will become rubbery.

Enokitake mushrooms are tiny, with bud-like caps at the end of long, slender stems. To appreciate their crisp texture and sweet flavour, use them raw in salads.

SHALLOTS

Although they belong to the same family as garlic, leeks, chives and onions – and look suspiciously like baby onions – shallots are very much their own vegetable. Sometimes called bunching onions, they have bulbs that multiply to produce clusters joined at the root end.

Shallots tend to be sweeter and much milder than large onions. Some Thai varieties are sweet enough to be used in desserts.

Indispensable in South-east Asian kitchens, shallots are far more popular than both regular onions and spring onions (scallions) for everyday use. Ground with garlic, ginger and other aromatics, shallots form the standard marinade and are also an essential ingredient in curry pastes and satay sauce. Dried shallots (hanh huong) are a popular alternative in Vietnam.

Preparation and cooking techniques: Trim the shallots, peel off the skin, then prise the bulbs apart. Leave these whole for braising, or chop as required. Thinly-sliced shallot rings are sometimes dry-fried until crisp, then used as a garnish.

Shallots will keep for several months in a cool, dry place.

FRUIT, NUTS AND SEEDS

If you are embarking on a low-fat eating plan, it can be all too easy to concentrate solely on the fat content of foods while ignoring the amount of sugar they contain. Avoid following a sensible main course with a sugary dessert. Instead, end a meal with a piece of fresh fruit or a few nuts. Fresh fruit, nuts and seeds are often used to flavour many Thai curries and other dishes.

LYCHEES

These moist fruits need no preparation once you have cracked the shells and peeled off the scaly red skin. The pearly white flesh inside can be sliced and used in a fruit salad or savoury dish. South-east Asian cooks like to pair lychees with pork. For a delectable sorbet, try puréed lychees with elderflower syrup. When buying fresh lychees, choose ones with pink or red shells; brown fruit are past their prime.

PINEAPPLES

The raw fruit and juice are very popular in Thailand, but pineapple is also used in cooked sweet and savoury dishes. Fresh pineapple will keep in a cool place for up to a week. To prepare pineapple, cut off the leaves, then quarter lengthways or cut in slices. Remove the skin and "eyes".

MANGOES

Most mangoes are oval in shape with blushed gold or pink skin. The easiest way to obtain mango chunks is to cut a thick lengthways slice off each side of the unpeeled fruit. Score the flesh on each slice with criss-cross lines. Fold these slices inside out and slice off the flesh.

PAPAYAS

Papayas or paw-paws can be small and round, but are usually pear-shaped. When ripe, the flesh is eaten as it is or used in fruit salads and other desserts. Papayas that are not too ripe can be added to soups, curries or seafood dishes. Unripe green papayas are served raw in salads and made into pickles. The juice and skins are used to tenderize meat.

LIME

These small, green and very sour citrus fruits are used extensively throughout the region. Fresh lime juice is served as a drink, with salt and sugar, and is also used in salad dressings.

COCONUT MILK AND CREAM

Coconut milk is high in fat but there is a version that is 88 per cent fat free. Coconut milk and cream are both made from the grated flesh of the coconut, and in the East, one can buy bags of freshly grated coconut for just this purpose. Warm water is added and the coconut is squeezed until the mixture is cloudy. When strained, this is coconut milk. If the milk is left to stand, coconut cream will float to the surface.

Left: Canned and fresh lychees have a wonderful scented aroma.

STAR FRUIT

The correct name for this fruit is carambola. Cylindrical in shape, the bright yellow waxy-looking fruit has five distinctive "wings" or protuberances which form the points of the star shapes revealed when the fruit is sliced. The flavour varies: fruits picked straight from the tree in Asia are inevitably sweet and scented, but those that have travelled long distances in cold storage can be disappointing.

PEANUTS

One of the most important flavourings in Thai cooking, peanuts are not especially low in fat but a small amount can make all the difference to the character of a dish. Raw peanuts have little smell, but once cooked they have a powerful aroma, a crunchy texture and a distinctive flavour. Peanuts play an important role in Asian cuisine. The smaller ones are used for making oil, while the larger, less oily nuts are widely eaten, both as a snack food and as ingredients in salads and main courses.

SESAME SEEDS

These tiny seeds are flat and pear-shaped. Raw sesame seeds have very little aroma and they are almost tasteless until they are roasted or dry-fried, which brings out their distinctive nutty flavour and aroma.

LOTUS SEEDS

Fresh lotus seeds are used as a snack food. The dried seeds must be soaked in water before use. The seeds are prized for their texture and ability to absorb other flavours. They are often added to soups.

HERBS AND SPICES

The principal flavourings favoured in South-east Asia have made a tremendous contribution to global cuisine. Ingredients like fresh ginger, lemon grass and kaffir lime now feature on menus the world over, not just in recipes that reflect their origin, but also in fusion food. Fish sauce is an essential seasoning for Thai and Vietnamese cooking, in much the same way that soy sauce is important to the Chinese and Japanese.

GARLIC

Often used with spring onions (scallions) and ginger, garlic is a vital ingredient in Thai and South-east Asian dishes. The most common variety has a purple skin, a fairly distinctive aroma and a hint of sweetness. Garlic may dominate a dish, but it may also impart a mild flavour, as when a garlic clove is heated in oil and then removed from the pan.

GALANGAL

Galangal is slightly harder than ginger, but used in much the same way. When young, the skin is creamy white with pink sprouts and the flavour is lemony. As galangal matures, the flavour intensifies and becomes more peppery.

GINGER

Valued not just as an aromatic, but also for its medicinal qualities, ginger is used throughout Asia. When young, ginger is juicy and tender, with a sharp flavour suggestive of citrus. At this stage it can easily be sliced, chopped or pounded to a paste. Older roots are tougher and may need to be peeled and grated. Pickled ginger is delicious. It can be served as a side dish, or combined with other ingredients such as beef or duck.

CHILLIES

Although they did not originate in South-east Asia, chillies have been embraced so fervently by Thailand that they are now irrevocably associated with the area. They are an essential ingredient in a variety of South-east Asian cuisines. But it is for their flavour rather than their fire that they are most valued. Be careful when you handle chillies. They contain a substance called capsaicin, which is a powerful irritant. If this comes into contact with delicate skin or the eyes, it can cause considerable pain. Wear gloves when handling chillies or wash your hands thoroughly in hot soapy water afterwards.

LEMON GRASS

A perennial tufted plant with a bulbous base, lemon grass looks like a plump spring onion (scallion). When the stalk is cut or bruised, the lively citrus aroma becomes evident. There are two main ways of using lemon grass. The stalk can be kept whole, bruised, then cooked slowly in liquid until it releases its flavour and is removed, or the tender lower portion of the stalk can be sliced or finely chopped and then stir-fried.

KAFFIR LIME LEAVES

These fruit are not true limes, but belong to a subspecies of the citrus family. Native to South-east Asia, they have green knobbly skins. The fruit is not edible, but the rind is sometimes used

Left: Red and green chillies

in cooking, but it is the leaves that are most highly prized. Kaffir lime leaves are synonymous with Thai cooking. The leaves are torn or finely shredded and used in soups and curries. Finely grated rind is added to fish or chicken dishes.

BASIL

Three types of basil are grown in Thailand, each with a slightly different appearance, flavour and use. Thai basil has a sweet, anise flavour and is used in red curries. Holy basil is pungent and tastes like cloves. Lemon basil is used in soups and is sprinkled on salads.

CORIANDER/CILANTRO

The entire coriander plant is used in Thai cooking – roots, stems, leaves and seeds. The fresh, delicate leaves are used in sauces, curries and for garnishes. The roots and stems are crushed and used for marinades. The seeds are ground to add flavour to various curry pastes.

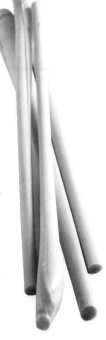

Above: Lemon grass

FISH SAUCE

Thai *nam pla* or fish sauce has a slightly stronger flavour and aroma than the Vietnamese or Chinese versions. It is used in Asia as a seasoning in all kinds of savoury dishes. It is also blended with extra flavourings such as finely chopped garlic and chillies, and sugar and lime juice to make a dipping sauce.

CURRY PASTES

Most Thai curries are based on "wet" spice mixtures, made by grinding spices and aromatics in a heavy mortar with a rough surface. Red curry paste is used in beef dishes and robust chicken dishes. Green curry paste, made from herbs and fresh green chillies, is used for chicken curries. Yellow curry paste and, the mildest of all, Mussaman curry paste are used for chicken and beef curries.

RICE

This low-fat high carbohydrate food is immensely important in Thai and South-east Asian cooking. When Thais are called to the table, the phrase used – *gkin kao* – literally translates as "a time to eat rice". All the other foods that make up a meal – meat, fish and vegetables – are regarded as accompaniments and are referred to as *ghap kao* or "things eaten with rice".

Rice is a non-allergenic food, rich in complex carbohydrates and low in salts and fats. It contains small amounts of easily digestible protein, together with phosphorous, magnesium, potassium and zinc. Brown rice, which retains the bran, yields vitamin E and some B-group vitamins, and is also a source of fibre. Although it is healthier than white rice, it is the latter that is preferred in South-east Asia.

The average Thai eats 158kg/350lb of rice every year, which is almost a pound a day. It is consumed in various forms, from basic steamed rice to rice noodles, crackers and cakes.

Two distinct types of rice are popular in Thailand. The first is a delicately scented long grain variety, which is used as a staple with all meals. It comes in several qualities, and is white and fluffy with separate grains when cooked. In northern Thailand, a starchy glutinous rice is preferred. When cooked, the grains stick together.

There are thousands of varieties of rice, many of which are known only in the areas where they are cultivated. The simplest method of classification is by the length of the grain, which can be long, medium or short. Long grain rice is three or four times as long as it is wide.

Above: Jasmine or Thai fragrant rice has tender, aromatic grains and is popular throughout central and southern Thailand and much of South-east Asia. It is widely available in supermarkets and Asian stores in the West.

JASMINE RICE

Also known as fragrant or scented rice, this long grain variety is the staple food of the central and southern parts of Thailand. As the name suggests, jasmine rice has a delicate aroma. The flavour is slightly nutty, and it resembles Basmati rice from India. The uncooked grains are translucent and, when cooked, the rice is fluffy and white. Most of the crop comes from a region between central and north-eastern Thailand where the soil is a combination of clay and sand. Newly harvested rice from this region is prized for the delicate texture of the grains.

GLUTINOUS RICE

Commonly referred to as sweet or sticky rice, glutinous rice is the mainstay of the diet in the northern and north-eastern regions of Thailand. It is delicious and very filling. The name is derived entirely from its sticky texture, as rice does not contain any gluten. Easily cultivated on the hillsides and high plateaux of these regions, glutinous rice requires less water during the growing period than the wet rice of the central lowlands.

Glutinous rice comes in both short or round grain and long grain varieties. Thai people prefer the long grain

Below: Glutinous rice, which may be black (although, more accurately, it is a very dark red), white or a hybrid known as "jasmine sweet", is most widely used in north and north-east Thailand.

Rice Mother
The traditional rice-growing communities in Thailand have a high regard for *Mae Pra Posop*, the "Rice Mother". Elaborate ceremonies are performed in her name during various stages of rice cultivation so that she may bless the fields with bountiful harvests from year to year.

Above: Rice is best cooked using the absorption method. Cook the rice with water in a tightly covered pan, then leave for 5 minutes until tender before serving.

variety; the short grain rice is more commonly used in Japanese and Chinese cooking. Some of the long grain varieties have a delicate, aromatic flavour, and these high-grade hybrids are sometimes labelled "jasmine sweet" or "jasmine glutinous rice", the adjective "jasmine" echoing the description used for their fragrant cousins in the non-glutinous rice family.

What makes this type of rice unusual is the way in which the grains clump together when cooked, enabling it to be eaten with the hands. Bitesize chunks of cooked rice are pulled off, one at a time, and rolled to a ball between the fingers and palm of the right hand. The ball is then dunked in a sauce or stew before being eaten. The process is not as messy as it sounds; if it is done correctly, then the grains stick to each other but not to the fingers or the palm. At the end of a meal, rolling the last piece of rice can actually have a cleansing effect, as the rice mops up any remaining juices or grease on the hand.

The starchiness of glutinous rice gives the uncooked grain a distinct opaque white colour, which is different from the more translucent appearance of regular rice grains. When soaked and steamed, however, the reverse is true. Glutinous rice becomes translucent, while regular rice turns opaque.

Although it is in the north and the north-eastern regions of Thailand that glutinous rice is most popular, it is also eaten elsewhere in the country, most frequently in sweet snacks or desserts. The rice is sweetened and flavoured with coconut milk, and is especially popular in the mango and durian season, when huge amounts of the coconut-flavoured rice are sold to eat with these precious fruits. Use low-fat coconut milk to keep the fat content as low as possible.

BLACK GLUTINOUS RICE

This wholegrain rice – that is, with only the husk removed – has a rich, nutty flavour that is distinctly different from the more subtle taste of white glutinous rice. It is generally sweetened with coconut milk and sugar and eaten as a snack or dessert, rather than being used as the staple of a savoury meal. Reduced-fat coconut milk makes an excellent substitute. It does tend to be quite heavy, filling and indigestible if eaten in quantity, so it is usually nibbled as a sweetmeat snack in the mid-afternoon or later in the evening, after the evening meal has been digested. A popular version of roasted glutinous rice, flattened into a cake, is *khao mow rang*, which is sold at all markets throughout Thailand.

In spite of its name, black rice isn't actually black in colour. If the grains are soaked in water for a few hours, the water will turn a deep burgundy red, showing the rice's true colour.

RICE PRODUCTS

Throughout Thailand and South-east Asia, rice, the staple carbohydrate, is used in many different ways.

Rice Flour

This flour may be made from either glutinous or non-glutinous raw rice that has been very finely ground. It is used to make the dough for fresh rice noodles and is also used to make

Above: Rice flour is finely ground and thoroughly pulverized. As a result, it has a very light texture and is used for fresh rice noodles.

desserts such as pancakes. Rice flour is readily available in Asian food stores. When the source is non-glutinous rice it is called *paeng khao jao* and when it is made from glutinous rice it is known as *paeng khao niao*. Store it as you would wheat flour.

Fermented Rice

Made by fermenting cooked glutinous rice, this is a popular sweetmeat, sold on market stalls and by street vendors.

Rice-pot Crust

In several cultures, the crust that forms on the base of the pan when rice is cooked in a particular way is highly prized. In Thailand, the crust is lifted off the base of the pan in sheets and is then dried out in the sun before being sold. *Khao tang* is lightly toasted or fried before being eaten.

To make *khao tang* at home, spread a layer of cooked rice about 5mm/¼in thick on a lightly greased baking sheet. Dry it out in a low oven, 140°C/275°F/ Gas 1, for several hours. Leave to cool, then break into pieces. Deep-fry for just a few seconds until puffed, but not browned. Lift out using a slotted spoon and drain on kitchen paper.

NOODLES AND WRAPPERS

Second only to rice in importance in the Thai diet, noodles and wrappers are cooked in a vast number of ways. Noodles are eaten at any time of day, including breakfast, and if hunger strikes unexpectedly, one of the many roadside noodle carts will furnish a tasty snack. For the local population, soup noodles are easily the most popular dish, but tourists tend to plump for *Pad Thai* (fried noodles). Wrappers are wrapped around all kinds of fillings.

NOODLES

There are basically five main varieties of noodles used in Thai cooking: *sen ya*, *ba mee*, *sen mee*, *sen lek* and *wun sen*. Most can be bought fresh in Asian stores, but it is more likely that you will find them dried. Noodles come in several sizes, from tiny transparent threads to large sheets. Many of them are made from rice, which serves to further emphasize the importance of the grain in the Thai diet. Other types of noodles are based on wheat flour or flour made from ground mung beans.

Unfortunately, the names of noodles are not standardized and the same type of noodle may go under several different names, depending on the manufacturer or which part of the country they come from. Noodles made without eggs are often labelled "imitation noodles" or "alimentary paste".

Noodle know-how
Both dried and fresh noodles have to be cooked in boiling water before use – or soaked in boiling water until pliable. How long for depends on the type of noodle, their thickness and whether or not the noodles are going to be cooked again in a soup or sauce. As a rule, once they have been soaked, dried noodles require about 3 minutes' cooking, while fresh ones will often be ready in less than a minute and may need to be rinsed under cold water to prevent them from overcooking.

Below: Dried vermicelli rice noodles should be soaked, not boiled.

RICE NOODLES

Both fresh and dried rice noodles are available in Asian supermarkets as well as in most large food stores. Fresh noodles are highly perishable, and they must be cooked as soon as possible after purchase. Rice noodles are available in a wide range of shapes and widths from fine vermicelli to medium rice noodle nests.

Vermicelli Rice Noodles

These noodles are usually sold dried and must be soaked in boiling water before use. When dried, rice vermicelli are known as rice stick noodles and rice river noodles, these noodles are sold both dried and fresh, although the latter form is more popular. Fresh rice stick noodles tend to be rather sticky and need to be separated before being cooked.

Medium Rice Noodles

Resembling spaghetti, these noodles are usually sold dried. The city of Chanthaburi in Thailand is famous for *sen lek* noodles, which are sometimes called *Jantoboon* noodles after the nickname for the town.

Rice Noodle Nests

Although the Thai name of these fresh thick round rice noodles means Chinese noodles, these are actually a Thai speciality, made of rice flour. In the Lacquer Pavilion of Suan Pakkad Palace there is a panel showing the making of *khanom chine* as part of the preparations for the Buddha's last meal. *Khanom chine* are white and the strands are a little thicker than spaghetti. At most markets in Thailand, nests of these noodles are a familiar sight. They are sold freshly cooked. You buy them by the hundred nests and should allow four or five nests per person. Buy the cheaper ones, because they taste better although they are not so white as the more expensive noodle nests. Fresh noodles are highly perishable, so, even though they are cooked, it makes sense to buy them early in the day, and steam them again when you get them home.

Fresh noodles are delicious when served with *nam ya*, *nam prik*, *sow nam* and a variety of curries.

Below: Flat rice noodles are similar to Italian tagliatelle.

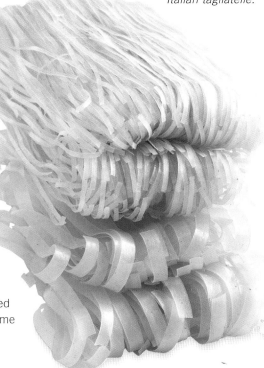

Preparing rice noodles is a simple matter. They need only to be soaked in hot water for a few minutes to soften them before serving. Add the noodles to a large bowl of just-boiled water and leave for 5–10 minutes, or until they soften, stirring occasionally to separate the strands. Their dry weight will usually double after soaking, so 115g/4oz dry noodles will produce about 225g/8oz after soaking.

Rice stick noodles puff up and become wonderfully crisp when they are deep-fried. Just a few deep-fried noodles sprinkled over a dish of boiled or reconstituted noodles will wonderfully enhance the flavour without seriously raising the fat content.

To prepare deep-fried rice noodles, place the noodles in a large mixing bowl and soak in cold water for 15 minutes. Drain them and lay them on kitchen paper to dry.

Then heat about 1.2 litres/2 pints/5 cups vegetable oil in a large, high-sided frying pan or wok to 180°C/350°F. To test if the oil is ready, carefully drop in a couple of noodle strands. If they puff and curl up immediately, the oil is hot enough. Very carefully, add a handful of dry noodles to the hot oil. As soon as they puff up, after about 2 seconds, flip

Below: Egg noodles are available, dried and fresh, in a wide variety of widths.

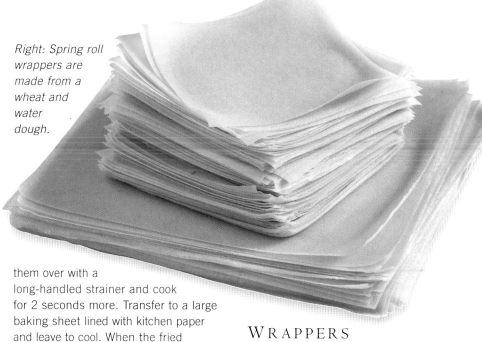

Right: Spring roll wrappers are made from a wheat and water dough.

them over with a long-handled strainer and cook for 2 seconds more. Transfer to a large baking sheet lined with kitchen paper and leave to cool. When the fried noodles are cold they can be transferred to a sealed plastic bag and will stay crisp for about 2 days.

EGG NOODLES

These noodles owe their yellow colour to the egg used in their manufacture. Sold fresh in nests, they must be shaken loose before being cooked. They come in both flat and round shapes. Very thin noodles are known as egg thread noodles. The flat type of noodles are generally used for soups and the rounded type are preferred for stir-frying. Egg noodles freeze well, provided that they are correctly wrapped. Thaw them thoroughly before using them in soup or noodles dishes.

Egg noodles should be cooked in boiling water for 4–5 minutes, or according to the packet instructions. Drain and serve.

CELLOPHANE NOODLES

These thin, wiry noodles, also called glass, jelly or bean thread noodles, are made from mung beans. They are the same size as ordinary egg noodles but they are transparent, resembling strips of cellophane or glass. They are only available dried.

Cellophane noodles are never served on their own, but always as an ingredient in a dish. Soak them in hot water for 10–15 minutes to soften them, then drain and cut into shorter strands.

WRAPPERS

These are made from wheat or rice flour and are used throughout Thailand and South-east Asia to wrap around a filling. Some may be eaten fresh while others are deep-fried.

WONTON WRAPPERS

Originally Chinese, these thin yellow pastry squares are made from egg and wheat flour and can be bought fresh or frozen. Fresh wrappers will last for about five days, double-wrapped and stored in the refrigerator. Simply peel off the number you require. Frozen wrappers should be thawed before use.

RICE PAPER

These brittle, semi-transparent, paper-thin sheets are made from a mixture of rice flour, water and salt, rolled out by a machine until very thin and then dried in the sun. Packets of 50–100 sheets are available. Store in a cool, dry place. Before use, dip in water until pliable, then wrap around a filling to make fresh spring rolls.

SPRING ROLL WRAPPERS

These wafer-thin wrappers are used to make classic spring rolls. The sizes available range from 8cm/3¼in to 30cm/12in square, and they usually come in packets of 20. Once opened, spring roll wrappers will dry out quickly, so peel off one at a time and keep the rest of the wrappers covered.

TOFU AND SOYA PRODUCTS

Tofu is a very versatile ingredient and, depending upon the texture, it can be cooked by almost every conceivable method, including stir-frying, steaming and poaching. It can be used with a vast array of ingredients, both sweet and savoury. As a low-fat ingredient, tofu is freely used as a meat replacement.

Made from soya beans, tofu (also widely known as beancurd) is popular throughout South-east Asia and one of the cheapest sources of protein in the world. Highly nutritious and low in fat and sugar, tofu is a much healthier food than either meat or fish, at a fraction of the cost. Tempeh is similar to tofu, but has a nuttier, more savoury flavour.

The nutritional value of tofu cannot be stressed too highly. As a vegetable protein, it contains the eight essential amino acids plus vitamins A and B. Tofu is free from cholesterol, and is regarded as an excellent food for anyone with heart disease or high blood pressure. In addition, it is very easy to digest, and this makes it an ideal food for infants, invalids and the elderly.

Although tofu is bland, it picks up the flavours of other foods when marinaded. It is important to cook it with such strongly flavoured seasonings as garlic, ginger, spring onions (scallions), chillies, soy sauce, oyster sauce, shrimp paste, fermented black beans, salted yellow beans, or sesame

oil. Tofu tastes very good with meat. It is often cooked with either pork or beef, but seldom with chicken. It goes well with fish and shellfish.

Two basic types of fresh tofu are widely available in the West: soft or silken tofu, and a firm type, called *momen*. Both kinds are creamy white in colour and are either packed in water or sold in vacuum packs. Several other tofu products are also popular in Thai and South-east Asian cooking.

PRESSED TOFU

This is a fresh bean curd cake that has had almost all the moisture squeezed out of it, leaving a solid block with a smooth texture. Brown outside and white inside, it is often seasoned with soy sauce and may also be smoked. You can press your own cakes of tofu by placing the bean curd between two plates. Weigh down the top one. Tilt the plates slightly to allow the liquid to drain off. Pressed tofu can be sliced and stir-fried.

DRIED BEAN CURD SKIN

This can also be purchased at Asian food stores. It consists of thin sheets of curd that are skimmed off simmering soya milk and dried. They are sold flat or rolled to form bean curd sticks. The skins can be used in casseroles, soups or stir-fries, and the sticks are popular in vegetarian dishes.

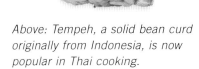

Above: Tempeh, a solid bean curd originally from Indonesia, is now popular in Thai cooking.

Dried bean curd skins need to be soaked in cold water before they can be used. The sheets require 1–2 hours, but the sticks should be soaked for several hours, preferably overnight.

DEEP-FRIED TOFU

Although deep-fried tofu is not especially low in fat, when used in small quantities it can significantly enhance the flavour of a dish without greatly increasing the fat content. When tofu is deep-fried in hot oil, it puffs up and turns golden brown, the flavour intensifies and the texture becomes chewy. Cubes of deep-fried tofu are sold in Asian markets. Store in the refrigerator and use within 3 days.

PICKLED TOFU OR BEAN PASTE

This product is made by fermenting fresh tofu, then drying it in the sun before marinating it in an alcohol mixture. The curd can be red or white and the flavour is extremely powerful. The best pickled bean curd comes from China and is sold in bottles or jars.

TEMPEH

This solid bean curd is an Indonesian speciality made by fermenting cooked soya beans with a cultured starter. It resembles firm tofu, but has a slightly nutty, more savoury taste. It benefits from a marinade.

Above: (clockwise from top) Pressed, silken and firm tofu. All are naturally low in fat and absorb the flavours of the ingredients with which they are cooked.

MEAT AND POULTRY

It is traditional in Thailand and South-east Asia for the meat element in a dish to be a relatively small percentage of the whole, with vegetables and noodles or rice making up the major portion. This is good news for anyone on a low-fat diet. When meat is included, it is usually used in stir-fries, soups and curries or grilled (broiled) dishes, none of which require much additional fat. Chicken is immensely popular and is the leanest meat. Pork, which comes a close second, is not quite such a healthy choice, although the breeding of new and leaner animals has reduced the fat content of pork in recent years. Lamb is not widely eaten, but there's a burgeoning interest in beef, partly because of the proliferation of fast-food restaurants in major cities.

Below: A whole raw chicken

CHICKEN

A whole chicken is a popular purchase almost everywhere in South-east Asia. The breast portion will be sliced or diced for a stir-fry; the rest of the meat will be carefully cut off the carcass and used in a red-cooked dish (when meat is slowly simmered in dark soy sauce to the dish a red tinge) or a curry and the bones will be simmered in water to make a stock or soup. The giblets are also valued, as are the feet.

DUCK

Much higher in saturated fat than chicken, especially if you eat the skin, duck is best kept for very occasional treats, or used in small quantities to flavour a substantial broth. When buying duck, look for a bird with a long body and a plump breast. The skin should be unmarked and should look creamy and slightly waxy. The healthiest way of cooking duck breast fillets is to steam them for about an hour, having first removed the skin. The meat can then be sliced and moistened with a little of the water from the steamer. Duck cooked this way is delicious in a salad.

PORK

The leanest cut of pork is fillet (tenderloin). There's very little waste with this cut, and it is perfect for stir-frying. Choose fillets that are pale pink all over. The flesh should be fairly firm, and should be slightly moist to the touch. Avoid any meat with discoloured areas. To prepare pork fillet, pull away the membrane that surrounds the meat, removing any fat at the same time. The sinew, which looks like a tougher strip of membrane, must be sliced away.

BEEF

In much of Thailand and South-east Asia, the cow was for many centuries regarded solely as a beast of burden, thus too precious to be slaughtered for food. Today, however, thanks to the fast-food industry, beef consumption is on the increase all over China, and even in Japan, which was for centuries a Buddhist (and therefore vegetarian) culture. When buying beef, look for deep red meat. For slow-cooked dishes, a generous marbling of fat is required, but if the meat is to be stir-fried, a leaner cut such as fillet (tenderloin) or rump (round) steak should be used.

LAMB

Although not as popular as pork or beef, lamb is nevertheless an important ingredient in some classic Asian dishes, particularly those that originated in Mongolia or Tibet. Remove any visible fat before cooking, and use sparingly, padding out the meal with vegetables or carbohydrates.

Above: Choose lean meat and cut off any visible fat.

Gluten – an alternative protein

Also known as "mock meat", gluten is another excellent source of vegetarian protein. Gluten is made from a mixture of wheat flour, salt and water, from which all the starch has been washed out. What remains when this has been done is a sponge-like gluten. Its Chinese name literally means "muscle or sinew of flour".

Like tofu, gluten has no aroma nor flavour of its own, but it has a much firmer texture, and can be shaped, coloured and flavoured to resemble meat, poultry or fish.

Unlike tofu, which is often cooked with meat and fish, gluten is regarded as a pure Buddhist ingredient, and as such, no non-vegetarian item may be mixed with it. This does not prevent accomplished Asian cooks from using a bit of sleight of hand, however, and gluten is often used with tofu to produce dishes such as "mock chicken", "mock abalone", "vegetarian duck" or "Buddhist pork" – which are all said to look and taste very much like the real thing.

Although gluten can be made at home, the task is too time-consuming to contemplate. Flavoured and cooked gluten is available in cans from Asian stores. It only needs to be reheated before being served.

Once opened, it will keep in the refrigerator for up to a week.

FISH AND SHELLFISH

Fish is an extremely important source of protein throughout Thailand and South-east Asia, whose many coastal waters, rivers and lakes provide an abundant harvest. From a healthy eating perspective, bass and sea bass, cod, sea bream, sole and plaice are excellent low-fat protein foods, but the darker-fleshed oily fish like tuna, salmon, carp, trout, mackerel, sardines and herring excite even more interest to those in search of a healthy diet. The Omega-3 fatty acids these fish contain benefit the heart. Scientific research has proved that they can help lower cholesterol and triglyceride levels and reduce the risk of high blood pressure. Scallops and squid are also a good source of Omega-3 fatty acids, and these, along with prawns (shrimp), crab and clams are used to great effect by Thai and South-east Asian cooks, whether steamed, poached, baked or fried.

CARP

This freshwater fish is widely farmed in Asia. It has meaty, moist flesh that can taste a little muddy to those unfamiliar with the distinctive taste. When buying carp, ask the fishmonger to remove the scales and strong dorsal fins. A favourite way of cooking carp is to stuff it with ginger and spring onions (scallions) and serve it with a sweet pickle sauce.

Above: Lobster and scallops are good, low-fat health choices.

MUSSELS

This shellfish is widely used in Thai and Asian cooking. Farmed mussels are now readily available and they are usually relatively free of barnacles. They are generally sold in quantities of 1kg/2¼lb, sufficient for a main course for two or three people. Look for good-size specimens with glossy shells. Discard any that are not closed, or which fail to shut when tapped. Use the back of a short stout knife to scrape away any barnacles, pull away the hairy "beards", then wash the shellfish thoroughly. The best way to cook mussels is to steam them in a small amount of flavoured liquor in a large lidded pan for 3–4 minutes until the shells open. Use finely chopped fresh root ginger, lemon grass, torn lime leaves and some fish sauce to add flavouring to the mussels.

LOBSTER

This luxury shellfish is usually served as a restaurant dish. To cook a live lobster, put it in a pan of ice cold water, cover the pan tightly and bring the water to the boil. The shell will turn bright red and the flesh will be tender and succulent when the lobster is cooked. If you buy a ready-cooked lobster the tail should spring back into a curl when pulled out straight. Try eating lobster with a dip of soy sauce with grated ginger.

Right from top: Freshwater carp, mackerel and grey mullet.

SALMON

The finest wild salmon has a superb flavour and is an excellent low-fat choice being full of Omega-3 acids. It is a costly fish, however, and so it may not be affordable on a regular basis. Responsibly farmed salmon is more economical to buy, and although the flavour is not quite as good as that of wild salmon, it is still delicious. The rosy flesh is beautifully moist and responds very well to being poached or baked, either on its own or with herbs and spices or aromatics. Salmon can take quite robust flavours. Try it with sweet soy sauce and noodles for a quick supper. When buying fresh salmon, have a good fishmonger cut you a chunk from a large salmon for really excellent results; do not use ready-cut steaks.

CRAB

Several varieties of crab are found in Asian waters. Off the coast of Vietnam and Cambodia, the saltwater variety can grow huge, at least 60cm/2ft in diameter. Crab meat has a distinctive taste that goes well with Thai and South-east Asian flavours. A popular Thai soup combines crab with asparagus, and a Vietnamese dish involves steaming lobster and crabs in beer.

Above: Raw, unshelled prawns

SCALLOPS

The tender, sweet flesh of this seafood needs very little cooking. Whenever possible, buy scallops fresh. If they are to be used for sashimi, the coral (roe), black stomach and frill must be removed first. In cooked dishes, the coral can be retained and is regarded as a delicacy.

SEA BASS

Characterized by the delicate flavour of its flesh, sea bass is enjoyed throughout Asia. It holds its shape when cooked, and can be grilled (broiled), steamed, baked or barbecued whole. Sea bass fillets taste delicious when they have been marinated, then cooked on a ridged griddle pan. Chunks or strips make a sensational stir-fry.

SHRIMPS AND PRAWNS

If you ask for shrimp in Britain, then you will be given tiny crustaceans, while in the United States, the term is used to describe the larger shellfish which the British refer to as prawns. However, Asian cooks use both words fairly

Right: Cooked prawns are a way of adding protein to a meal without adding fat.

indiscriminately, so check what a recipe requires. Buy raw shellfish whenever possible, and then cook it yourself. This applies to fresh and frozen mixed seafood. If the shellfish are frozen, thaw them slowly and pat them dry before cooking. Since they are low in fat, they are one of the healthiest forms of protein.

SQUID

The cardinal rule with squid is to either cook it very quickly, or simmer it for a long time. Anything in between will result in seafood that is tough and rubbery. Squid is an ideal candidate for stir-frying with flavours like ginger, garlic, spring onion (scallion) and chilli, and it will also make an interesting salad. For a slow-cooked dish, try squid cooked in a clay pot with chillies and noodles.

TUNA

This very large fish is usually sold as steaks, which can be pink or red, depending on the variety. Avoid steaks with heavy discoloration around the bone, or which are brownish and dull-looking. The flesh should be solid and compact. Tuna loses its colour and can become dry when overcooked, so cook it only briefly over high heat, or stew it gently with moist ingredients like tomatoes and peppers.

Fantail prawns/shrimp

1 Remove the heads from the prawns and peel away most of the body shell. Leave a little of the shell to keep the tail intact.

2 Make a tiny incision in the back of each prawn and remove the black intestinal cord.

3 Hold the prepared prawns by the tails and dip lightly in seasoned cornflour (cornstarch), and then in a frothy batter before cooking them in hot oil until the tails, which are free from batter, turn red.

Butterfly prawns/shrimp

Prawns (shrimp) prepared this way cook quickly and curl attractively.

1 Remove the heads and body shells, but leave the tails. Pull out the intestinal cords using tweezers.

2 Make a cut through the belly of each prawn.

3 Gently open out the two halves of the prawn so that they will look like butterfly wings.

FAT AND CALORIE CONTENTS

The figures show the weight of fat (g) and the energy content per 100g (3½oz) of each of the following typical foods used in Thai and South-east Asian cooking. Use the table to help work out the fat content of favourite dishes.

MEATS	fat (g)	Energy kcals/kJ
Beef minced (ground), raw	16.2	225kcal/934kJ
Beef, rump (round) steak, lean only	4.1	125kcal/526kJ
Beef, fillet (tenderloin) steak	8.5	191kcal/799kJ
Chicken, minced (ground), raw	8.5	106kcal/449kJ
Chicken fillet, raw	1.1	106kcal/449kJ
Chicken thighs, without skin, raw	6.0	126kcal/530kJ
Duck, without skin, cooked	9.5	182kcal/765kJ
Lamb leg, lean, cooked	6.3	198kcal/831kJ
Liver, lamb's, raw	6.2	137kcal/575kJ
Pork, average, lean, raw	4.0	123kcal/519kJ
Pork, lean roast	4.0	163kcal/685kJ
Pork, minced (ground), raw	4.0	123kcal/519kJ
Pork, ribs, raw	10.0	114kcal/480kJ
Turkey, meat only, raw	1.6	105kcal/443kJ
Turkey, minced (ground), raw	6.5	170kcal/715kJ

FISH AND SHELLFISH	fat (g)	Energy kcals/kJ
Cod, raw	0.7	80kcal/337kJ
Crab meat, raw	0.5	54kcal/230kJ
Mackerel, raw	16.0	221kcal/930kJ
Monkfish, raw	1.5	76kcal/320kJ
Mussels, raw, weight without shells	1.8	74kcal/312kJ
Mussels, raw, weight with shells	0.6	24kcal/98kJ
Oysters, raw	4.2	120kcal/508kJ
Prawns (shrimp)	1.0	76kcal/320kJ
Salmon, steamed	13.0	200kcal/837kJ
Scallops, raw	1.6	105kcal/440kJ
Sardine fillets, grilled	10.4	195kcal/815kJ
Sardines, grilled, weight with bones	6.3	19kcal/497kJ
Sea bass, raw	2.0	97kcal/406kJ
Squid, boiled	1.0	79kcal/330kJ
Swordfish, grilled	5.1	155kcal/649kJ
Tuna, grilled	6.3	184kcal/770kJ

VEGETABLES	fat (g)	Energy kcals/kJ
Asparagus	0.0	12.5kcal/52.5kJ
Aubergine (eggplant)	0.4	15kcal/63kJ
Bamboo shoots	0.0	29kcal/120kJ
Beansprouts	1.6	10kcal/42kJ
(Bell) peppers	0.4	32kcals/128kJ
Beans, fine green	0.0	7kcal/29kJ
Beetroot (beets)	0.1	36kcal/151kJ
Broccoli	0.9	33kcal/138kJ
Carrot	0.3	35kcal/156kJ
Celery	0.2	7kcal/142kJ
Chilli, fresh	0.0	30kcal/120kJ
Chinese leaves (Chinese cabbage)	0.0	8kcal/35kJ
Courgettes (zucchini)	0.4	18kcal74kJ
Cucumber	0.1	10kcal/40kJ
Leek	0.3	20kcal/87kJ
Lotus root, raw	0.0	74kcal/310kJ
Mangetouts (snow peas)	0.4	81kcal/339kJ
Mung beans, cooked	0.1	70kcal/295kJ
Mushrooms, button (white)	0.5	24kcal/100kJ
Mushrooms, shiitake	0.2	55kcal/230kJ
Mushrooms, dried	0.0	56kcal/240kJ
Onion	0.2	36kcal/151kJ
Pak choi (bok choy)	0.0	13kcal/53kJ
Spinach (fresh, cooked)	0.0	20kcal/87kJ
Spring onion (scallion)	0.0	17kcal/83kJ
Sweet potato (peeled, boiled)	0.0	84kcal/358kJ
Water chestnuts	0.0	98kcal/410kJ

NUTS AND SEEDS	fat (g)	Energy kcals/kJ
Cashew nuts	48.0	573kcal/2406kJ
Chestnuts	2.7	169kcal/714kJ
Peanuts	26.9	586kcal/2464kJ
Sesame seeds	47.0	507kcal/2113kJ

Below: Red meat such as beef, lamb and pork have a higher quantity of fat per 100g than white meat.

Below: Seafood is a good source of vitamins, minerals and protein. Oily fish contains high levels of Omega-3 fatty acids.

FRUIT	fat (g)	Energy kcals/kJ
Apples, eating	0.1	47kcal/199kJ
Bananas	0.3	95kcal/403kJ
Grapefruit	0.1	30kcal/126kJ
Grapes (green)	0.0	56kcal/235kJ
Lychees	0.1	58kcal/248kJ
Mangoes	0.0	60Kcal/251kJ
Nectarine	0.0	40kcal/169kJ
Oranges	0.1	37kcal/158kJ
Papayas	0	36kcal/153kJ
Peaches	0.0	31kcal/132kJ
Pineapple, fresh	0.0	50Kcal/209kJ
Pineapple, canned chunks	0.2	63Kcal/264kJ
Raspberries	0.0	28Kcal/117kJ
Star fruit (carambola)	0.0	25Kcal/105kJ
Strawberries	0.0	27kcal/113kJ
Watermelon	0.0	23kcal/95kJ

BEANS, NOODLES, RICE AND TOFU	fat (g)	Energy kcals/kJ
Aduki beans, cooked	0.2	123kcal/525kJ
Noodles, cellophane	trace	351kcal/1468kJ
Noodles, egg	0.5	62kcal/264kJ
Noodles, plain wheat	2.5	354kcal/1190kJ
Noodles, rice	0.1	360kcal/1506kJ
Noodles, soba	0.1	99kcal/414kJ
Rice, brown, uncooked	2.8	357kcal/1518kJ
Rice, white, uncooked	3.6	383kcal/1630kJ
Tofu, firm	4.2	73kcal/304kJ
Tofu, silken	2.5	55kcal/230kJ

BAKING AND PANTRY	fat (g)	Energy kcals/kJ
Cornflour (cornstarch)	0.7	354kcal/1508kJ
Flour, plain (all-purpose) white	1.3	341kcal/1450kJ
Flour, self-raising (self-rising)	1.2	330kcal/1407kJ
Flour, wholemeal (whole-wheat)	2.2	310kcal/1318kJ
Tapioca	0.0	28kcal/119kJ
Honey	0.0	288kcal/1229kJ
Soy sauce, per 5ml/1 tsp	0.0	9kcal/40kJ
Sugar, white	0.3	94kcal/1680kJ

FATS, OILS AND EGGS	fat (g)	Energy kcals/kJ
Butter	81.7	737kcal/3031kJ
Low-fat spread	40.5	390kcal/1605kJ
Very low-fat spread	25.0	273kcal/1128kJ
Oil, corn, per 1 tbsp/15ml	13.8	124kcal/511kJ
Oil, groundnut (peanut), per 1 tbsp/15ml	14.9	134kcal/552kJ
Oil, sesame seed, per 1 tbsp/15ml	14.9	134kcal/552kJ
Oil, sunflower, per 1 tbsp/15ml	13.8	124kcal/511kJ
Eggs	10.8	147kcal/612kJ
Coconut milk	17.0	225kcal/944kJ
Coconut milk, reduced-fat	8.6	137kcal/575kJ
Coconut cream	68.8	669kcal/2760kJ

DAIRY PRODUCTS	fat (g)	Energy kcals/kJ
Cheese, hard	34.4	412kcal/1708kJ
Cheese, hard, reduced fat	15.0	261kcal/1091kJ
Cheese, cottage	3.9	98kcal/413kJ
Cheese, cream	47.4	439kcal/1807kJ
Cream, double (heavy)	48.0	449kcal/1849kJ
Cream, reduced-fat double (heavy)	24.0	243kcal/1002kJ
Cream, single (light)	19.1	198kcal/817kJ
Cream, whipping	39.3	373kcal/1539kJ
Crème fraîche	40.0	379kcal/156kJ
Crème fraîche, reduced fat	15.0	165kcal/683kJ
Fromage frais, plain	7.1	113kcal/469kJ
Fromage frais, very low-fat	0.2	58kcal/247kJ
Milk, full cream (whole)	3.9	66kcal/275kJ
Milk, semi-skimmed (low-fat)	1.5	35kcal/146kJ
Milk, skimmed	0.1	33kcal/130kJ
Yogurt, low-fat natural (plain)	0.8	56kcal/236kJ
Yogurt, Greek (US strained plain)	9.1	115kcal/477kJ

Below: Vegetables are very low in fat. Eat them raw for a filling snack, or steam them to retain maximum nutritional value.

Below: Soya products, such as tofu, soya milk and soya beans, contain isoflavones that are thought to lower cholesterol levels.

Soups, Appetizers and Light Bites

Follow the low-fat recipes in this section and treat your party guests to such delicious healthy soups and appetizers as soothing Hot and Sweet Vegetable and Tofu Soup, fragrant Thai Fish Broth and crunchy Corn Fritters. Traditional street fare such as spring rolls and samosas can be amazingly low in cholesterol and prove a popular snack.

CELLOPHANE NOODLE SOUP ★

THE NOODLES USED IN THIS SOUP GO BY VARIOUS NAMES: GLASS NOODLES, CELLOPHANE NOODLES, BEAN THREAD OR TRANSPARENT NOODLES. THEY ARE ESPECIALLY VALUED FOR THEIR BRITTLE TEXTURE.

SERVES FOUR

INGREDIENTS
  4 large dried shiitake mushrooms
  15g/½oz dried golden needles
    (lily buds)
  ½ cucumber, coarsely chopped
  2 garlic cloves, halved
  90g/3½oz white cabbage, chopped
  1.2 litres/2 pints/5 cups boiling water
  115g/4oz cellophane noodles
  30ml/2 tbsp soy sauce
  15ml/1 tbsp palm sugar or light
    muscovado (brown) sugar
  90g/3½oz block silken tofu, diced
  fresh coriander (cilantro) leaves,
    to garnish

1 Soak the shiitake mushrooms in warm water for 30 minutes. In a separate bowl, soak the dried golden needles in warm water, also for 30 minutes.

2 Meanwhile, put the cucumber, garlic and cabbage in a food processor and process to a smooth paste. Scrape the mixture into a large pan and add the measured boiling water.

3 Bring to the boil, then reduce the heat and cook for 2 minutes, stirring occasionally. Strain this stock into another pan, return to a low heat and bring to simmering point.

4 Drain the golden needles, rinse under cold running water, then drain again. Cut off any hard ends. Add to the stock with the noodles, soy sauce and sugar and cook for 5 minutes more.

5 Strain the mushroom soaking liquid into the soup. Discard the mushroom stems, then slice the caps. Divide them and the tofu among four bowls. Pour the soup over, garnish and serve.

Energy 148kcal/618kJ; Protein 4.1g; Carbohydrate 29.7g, of which sugars 5.7g; Fat 1.1g, of which saturates 0.1g, of which polyunsaturates 0.5g; Cholesterol 0mg; Calcium 139mg; Fibre 0.7g; Sodium 546mg.

MIXED VEGETABLE SOUP ★

THIS TYPE OF SOUP IS USUALLY MADE IN LARGE QUANTITIES AND THEN REHEATED FOR CONSUMPTION OVER SEVERAL DAYS. IF YOU WOULD LIKE TO DO THE SAME, DOUBLE OR TREBLE THE QUANTITIES.

SERVES FOUR

INGREDIENTS

15ml/1 tbsp sunflower oil
15ml/1 tbsp magic paste (see Cook's Tip)
90g/3½oz Savoy cabbage or Chinese leaves (Chinese cabbage), finely shredded
90g/3½oz mooli (daikon), finely diced
1 medium cauliflower, coarsely chopped
4 celery sticks, coarsely chopped
1.2 litres/2 pints/5 cups vegetable stock
130g/4½oz fried tofu, cut into 2.5cm/1in cubes
5ml/1 tsp palm sugar or light muscovado (brown) sugar
45ml/3 tbsp light soy sauce

1 Heat the sunflower oil in a large, heavy pan or wok. Add the magic paste and cook over a low heat, stirring frequently, until it gives off its aroma. Add the shredded Savoy cabbage or Chinese leaves, mooli, cauliflower and celery. Pour in the vegetable stock, increase the heat to medium and bring to the boil, stirring occasionally. Gently stir in the tofu cubes.

2 Add the sugar and soy sauce. Reduce the heat and simmer for 15 minutes, until the vegetables are cooked and tender. Taste and add a little more soy sauce if needed. Serve hot.

COOK'S TIP
Magic paste is a mixture of crushed garlic, white pepper and coriander (cilantro). Look for it at Thai markets.

Energy 75kcal/311kJ; Protein 3.6g; Carbohydrate 4g, of which sugars 3.8g; Fat 5g, of which saturates 0.6g, of which polyunsaturates 3g; Cholesterol 0mg; Calcium 196mg; Fibre 1g; Sodium 825mg.

HOT AND SWEET VEGETABLE AND TOFU SOUP ★

AN INTERESTING COMBINATION OF HOT, SWEET AND SOUR FLAVOURS THAT MAKES FOR A SOOTHING, LOW-FAT SOUP. IT TAKES ONLY MINUTES TO MAKE AS THE SPINACH AND SILKEN TOFU ARE SIMPLY PLACED IN BOWLS AND COVERED WITH THE FLAVOURED HOT STOCK.

SERVES FOUR

INGREDIENTS
 1.2 litres/2 pints/5 cups
   vegetable stock
 5–10ml/1–2 tsp Thai red
   curry paste
 2 kaffir lime leaves, torn
 40g/1½oz/3 tbsp palm sugar or light
   muscovado (brown) sugar
 30ml/2 tbsp soy sauce
 juice of 1 lime
 1 carrot, cut into thin batons
 50g/2oz baby spinach leaves, any
   coarse stalks removed
 225g/8oz block silken tofu, diced

1 Heat the stock in a large pan, then add the red curry paste. Stir constantly over a medium heat until the paste has dissolved. Add the lime leaves, sugar and soy sauce and bring to the boil.

2 Add the lime juice and carrot to the pan. Reduce the heat and simmer for 5–10 minutes. Place the spinach and tofu in four individual serving bowls and pour the hot stock on top to serve.

Energy 98kcal/412kJ; Protein 5.3g; Carbohydrate 12.7g, of which sugars 12.3g; Fat 3.3g, of which saturates 0.4g, of which polyunsaturates 1.7g; Cholesterol 0mg; Calcium 318mg; Fibre 0.6g; Sodium 558mg.

BROTH <u>WITH</u> STUFFED CABBAGE LEAVES ★

A SUBTLY SPICY FILLING OF PRAWNS, PORK AND VEGETABLES IS FLAVOURED WITH TRADITIONAL THAI INGREDIENTS. THE HEALTHY LOW-FAT FILLING IS WRAPPED IN CABBAGE LEAVES AND SIMMERED IN A WONDERFULLY AROMATIC CHICKEN STOCK FOR FULL FLAVOUR WITHOUT FAT.

SERVES FOUR

INGREDIENTS

   10 Chinese leaves (Chinese cabbage)
     or Savoy cabbage leaves, halved,
     main ribs removed
   4 spring onions (scallions),
     green tops left whole, white
     part finely chopped
   5–6 dried cloud ear (wood ear)
     mushrooms, soaked in hot water
     for 15 minutes
   115g/4oz minced (ground) lean pork
   115g/4oz prawns (shrimp), shelled,
     deveined and finely chopped
   1 Thai chilli, seeded and chopped
   30ml/2 tbsp *nuoc mam*
   15ml/1 tbsp soy sauce
   4cm/1½in fresh root ginger, peeled
     and very finely sliced
   chopped fresh coriander (cilantro),
     to garnish
For the stock
   1 meaty chicken carcass
   2 onions, peeled and quartered
   4 garlic cloves, crushed
   4cm/1½in fresh root ginger,
     chopped
   30ml/2 tbsp *nuoc mam*
   30ml/2 tbsp soy sauce
   6 black peppercorns
   a few sprigs of fresh thyme
   sea salt

1 To make the chicken stock, put the chicken carcass into a deep pan. Add all the other stock ingredients except the sea salt and pour over 2 litres/3½ pints/8 cups of water. Bring to the boil, and boil for a few minutes, skim off any foam, then reduce the heat and simmer gently with the lid on for 1½–2 hours.

2 Remove the lid and simmer for a further 30 minutes to reduce the stock. Skim off any fat, season with sea salt, then strain the stock and measure out 1.5 litres/2½ pints/6¼ cups. It is important to skim off any froth or fat, so that the broth is light and fragrant.

3 Blanch the cabbage leaves in boiling water for about 2 minutes, or until tender. Remove with a slotted spoon and refresh under cold water. Add the green tops of the spring onions to the boiling water and blanch for a minute, or until tender, then drain and refresh under cold water. Carefully tear each piece into five thin strips and set aside.

4 Squeeze dry the cloud ear mushrooms, then trim and finely chop and mix with the pork, prawns, spring onion whites, chilli, *nuoc mam* and soy sauce. Lay a cabbage leaf flat on a surface and place a teaspoon of the filling about 1cm/½in from the bottom edge – the edge nearest to you.

5 Fold this bottom edge over the filling, and then fold in the sides of the leaf to seal it. Roll all the way to the top of the leaf to form a tight bundle. Wrap a piece of blanched spring onion green around the bundle and tie it so that it holds together. Repeat with the remaining leaves and filling.

6 Bring the stock to the boil in a wok or deep pan. Stir in the finely sliced ginger, then reduce the heat and drop in the cabbage bundles. Bubble very gently over a low heat for about 20 minutes to ensure that the filling is thoroughly cooked. Serve immediately, ladled into bowls with a sprinkling of fresh coriander leaves.

Energy 80kcal/334kJ; Protein 12.7g; Carbohydrate 3.9g, of which sugars 3.7g; Fat 1.5g, of which saturates 0.5g, of which polyunsaturates 0.4g; Cholesterol 74mg; Calcium 68mg; Fibre 1.4g; Sodium 891mg.

PUMPKIN AND COCONUT SOUP ★

IN THIS LOVELY LOOKING SOUP, THE NATURAL SWEETNESS OF THE PUMPKIN IS HEIGHTENED BY THE ADDITION OF A LITTLE SUGAR, BUT THIS IS BALANCED BY THE CHILLIES, SHRIMP PASTE AND DRIED SHRIMP. REDUCED-FAT COCONUT MILK BLURS THE BOUNDARIES BEAUTIFULLY.

SERVES SIX

INGREDIENTS
   450g/1lb pumpkin
   2 garlic cloves, crushed
   4 shallots, finely chopped
   2.5ml/½ tsp shrimp paste
   1 lemon grass stalk, chopped
   2 fresh green chillies, seeded
   15ml/1 tbsp dried shrimp soaked
      for 10 minutes in warm water
      to cover
   600ml/1 pint/2½ cups
      chicken stock
   600ml/1 pint/2½ cups reduced-fat
      coconut milk
   30ml/2 tbsp Thai fish sauce
   5ml/1 tsp granulated sugar
   115g/4oz small cooked shelled
      prawns (shrimp)
   salt and ground black pepper
To garnish
   2 fresh red chillies, seeded and
      thinly sliced
   10–12 fresh basil leaves

1 Peel the pumpkin and cut it into quarters with a sharp knife. Scoop out the seeds with a teaspoon and discard. Cut the flesh into chunks about 2cm/¾in thick and set aside.

2 Put the garlic, shallots, shrimp paste, lemon grass, green chillies and salt to taste in a mortar. Drain the dried shrimp, discarding the soaking liquid, and add them, then use a pestle to grind the mixture into a paste. Alternatively, place all the ingredients in a food processor and process to a paste.

3 Bring the chicken stock to the boil in a large pan. Add the ground paste and stir well to dissolve.

4 Add the pumpkin chunks and bring to a simmer. Simmer for 10–15 minutes, or until the pumpkin is tender.

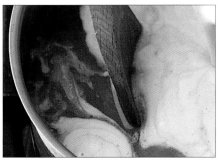

5 Stir in the coconut milk, then bring the soup back to simmering point. Do not let it boil. Add the fish sauce, sugar and ground black pepper to taste.

6 Add the prawns and cook for a further 2–3 minutes, until they are heated through. Serve in warm soup bowls, garnished with chillies and basil leaves.

COOK'S TIP
Shrimp paste is made from ground shrimp fermented in brine.

Energy 63kcal/269kJ; Protein 6g; Carbohydrate 9g, of which sugars 8.2g; Fat 0.7g, of which saturates 0.3g, of which polyunsaturates 0.1g; Cholesterol 50mg; Calcium 101mg; Fibre 1g; Sodium 611mg.

NORTHERN PRAWN AND SQUASH SOUP ★

AS THE TITLE OF THE RECIPE SUGGESTS, THIS COMES FROM NORTHERN THAILAND. IT IS QUITE HEARTY, SOMETHING OF A CROSS BETWEEN A SOUP AND A STEW. THE BANANA FLOWER ISN'T ESSENTIAL, BUT IT DOES ADD A UNIQUE AND AUTHENTIC FLAVOUR.

SERVES FOUR

INGREDIENTS

   1 butternut squash, about 300g/11oz
   1 litre/1¾ pints/4 cups
     vegetable stock
   90g/3½oz/scant 1 cup green beans,
     cut into 2.5cm/1in pieces
   45g/1¾oz dried banana
     flower (optional)
   15ml/1 tbsp Thai fish sauce
   225g/8oz raw prawns (shrimp)
   small bunch fresh basil
   cooked rice, to serve
For the chilli paste
   115g/4oz shallots, sliced
   10 drained bottled green peppercorns
   1 small fresh green chilli, seeded and
     finely chopped
   2.5ml/½ tsp shrimp paste

1 Peel the squash and cut it in half. Scoop out the seeds and discard, then cut the flesh into neat cubes. Set aside.

2 Make the chilli paste by pounding the sliced shallots, peppercorns, chilli and shrimp paste together using a mortar and pestle or puréeing them in a spice blender.

3 Heat the **vegetable** stock gently in a large pan, then stir in the chilli paste. Add the squash, beans and banana flower, if using. Bring to the boil and cook for 15 minutes.

4 Add the fish sauce, prawns and basil. Simmer for 3 minutes. Serve in warmed bowls, accompanied by rice.

Energy 73kcal/307kJ; Protein 11.8g; Carbohydrate 5.2g, of which sugars 3.9g; Fat 0.7g, of which saturates 0.2g, of which polyunsaturates 0.2g; Cholesterol 113mg; Calcium 90mg; Fibre 1.7g; Sodium 669mg.

THAI FISH BROTH ★

LEMON GRASS, CHILLIES AND GALANGAL ARE AMONG THE FLAVOURINGS USED IN THIS FRAGRANT SOUP.

SERVES THREE

INGREDIENTS

  1 litre/1¾ pints/4 cups fish or
    light chicken stock
  4 lemon grass stalks
  3 limes
  2 small fresh hot red chillies,
    seeded and thinly sliced
  2cm/¾in piece fresh galangal,
    peeled and thinly sliced
  6 fresh coriander (cilantro) stalks
  2 kaffir lime leaves, finely
    chopped
  350g/12oz monkfish fillet, skinned
    and cut into 2.5cm/1in pieces
  15ml/1 tbsp rice vinegar
  45ml/3 tbsp Thai fish sauce
  30ml/2 tbsp chopped coriander
    (cilantro) leaves, to garnish

1 Pour the stock into a pan and bring it to the boil. Meanwhile, slice the bulb end of each lemon grass stalk diagonally into pieces about 3mm/⅛in thick. Peel off four wide strips of lime rind with a potato peeler, taking care to avoid the white pith underneath which would make the soup bitter. Squeeze the limes and reserve the juice.

2 Add the sliced lemon grass, lime rind, chillies, galangal and coriander stalks to the stock, with the kaffir lime leaves. Simmer for 1–2 minutes.

VARIATIONS
Prawns (shrimp), scallops, squid or sole can be substituted for the monkfish. If you use kaffir lime leaves, you will need the juice of only 2 limes.

3 Add the monkfish, rice vinegar and Thai fish sauce, with half the reserved lime juice. Simmer for about 3 minutes, until the fish is just cooked. Lift out and discard the coriander stalks, taste the broth and add more lime juice if necessary; the soup should taste quite sour. Sprinkle with the coriander leaves and serve very hot.

Energy 88kcal/373kJ; Protein 19.2g; Carbohydrate 1.5g, of which sugars 1.3g; Fat 0.6g, of which saturates 0.1g, of which polyunsaturates 0.2g; Cholesterol 16mg; Calcium 40mg; Fibre 0.4g; Sodium 1112mg

HOT-AND-SOUR FISH SOUP ★

CHILLIES PROVIDE THE HEAT, TAMARIND THE TARTNESS AND THE SWEETNESS COMES FROM PINEAPPLE.

SERVES FOUR

INGREDIENTS

  1 catfish, sea bass or red snapper,
    about 1kg/2¼lb, filleted
  60–75ml/4–5 tbsp *nuoc mam* or
    other fish sauce
  2 garlic cloves, finely chopped
  25g/1oz dried squid, soaked
    in water for 30 minutes
  10ml/2 tsp vegetable oil
  2 spring onions (scallions), sliced
  2 shallots, sliced
  4cm/1½in fresh root ginger, peeled
    and chopped
  2–3 lemon grass stalks, cut into
    strips and crushed
  30ml/2 tbsp tamarind paste
  2–3 Thai chillies, seeded
    and sliced
  15ml/1 tbsp sugar
  225g/8oz fresh pineapple, peeled
    and diced
  3 tomatoes, skinned, seeded and
    roughly chopped
  50g/2oz canned sliced bamboo
    shoots, drained
  1 small bunch fresh coriander
    (cilantro), stalks removed, leaves
    finely chopped
  salt and ground black pepper
  115g/4oz/½cup beansprouts and
    1 bunch dill, fronds roughly
    chopped, to garnish
  1 lime, cut into quarters, to serve

1 Cut the fish into bitesize pieces, mix with 30ml/2 tbsp of the *nuoc mam* or other fish sauce with garlic and leave to marinate. Save the head, tail and bones for the stock. Drain and rinse the soaked dried squid.

2 Heat the oil in a deep pan and stir in the spring onions, shallots, ginger, lemon grass and dried squid. Add the reserved fish head, tail and bones, and sauté them gently for a minute or two. Pour in 1.2 litres/2 pints/5 cups water and bring to the boil. Reduce the heat and simmer for 30 minutes.

3 Strain the stock into another deep pan and bring to the boil. Stir in the tamarind paste, chillies, sugar and the remaining *nuoc mam* and simmer for 2–3 minutes. Add the pineapple, tomatoes and bamboo shoots and simmer for a further 2–3 minutes. Stir in the fish pieces and the chopped fresh coriander, and cook until the fish turns opaque.

4 Season to taste and ladle the soup into hot bowls. Garnish with beansprouts and dill, and serve with the lime quarters to squeeze over.

VARIATIONS

• Depending on your mood, or your palate, you can adjust the balance of hot and sour by adding more chilli or tamarind to taste. Enjoyed as a meal in itself, the soup is usually served with plain steamed rice but in Ho Chi Minh City in Vietnam it is served with chunks of fresh baguette, which are perfect for soaking up the spicy, fruity, tangy broth.
• Other fresh herbs, such as chopped mint and basil leaves, also complement this soup.

Energy 166kcal/704kJ; Protein 23.1g; Carbohydrate 10.9g, of which sugars 10g; Fat 3.7g, of which saturates 0.6g, of which polyunsaturates 1.7g; Cholesterol 51mg; Calcium 113mg; Fibre 3g; Sodium 116mg.

AROMATIC BROTH WITH ROAST DUCK, PAK CHOI AND EGG NOODLES ★

SERVED ON ITS OWN, THIS CHINESE-INSPIRED DUCK AND NOODLE SOUP MAKES A DELICIOUS AUTUMN OR WINTER MEAL. IN A VIETNAMESE HOUSEHOLD, A BOWL OF WHOLE FRESH OR MARINATED CHILLIES MIGHT BE PRESENTED AS A FIERY SIDE DISH TO CHEW ON.

SERVES SIX

INGREDIENTS
    5ml/1 tsp sunflower oil
    2 shallots, thinly sliced
    4cm/1½ in fresh root ginger,
        peeled and sliced
    15ml/1 tbsp soy sauce
    5ml/1 tsp five-spice powder
    10ml/2 tsp sugar
    175g/6oz pak choi (bok choy)
    450g/1lb fresh egg noodles
    225g/8oz roast duck, thinly sliced
    sea salt
For the stock
    1 chicken carcass
    2 carrots, peeled and quartered
    2 onions, peeled and quartered
    4cm/1½ in fresh root ginger, peeled
        and cut into chunks
    2 lemon grass stalks, chopped
    30ml/2 tbsp *nuoc mam*
    15ml/1 tbsp soy sauce
    6 black peppercorns
For the garnish
    4 spring onions (scallions), sliced
    1–2 red Serrano chillies, seeded and
        finely sliced
    1 bunch each coriander (cilantro) and
        basil, stalks removed, leaves
        chopped

1 To make the stock, put the chicken carcass into a deep pan. Add all the other stock ingredients and pour in 2.5 litres/4½ pints/10¼ cups water. Bring to the boil, and boil for a few minutes, skim off any foam, then reduce the heat and simmer gently with the lid on for 2–3 hours. Remove the lid and continue to simmer for a further 30 minutes to reduce the stock. Skim off any fat, season with salt, then strain the stock. Measure out 2 litres/3½ pints/8 cups.

2 Heat the oil in a wok or deep pan and stir in the shallots and ginger. Add the soy sauce, five-spice powder, sugar and stock and bring to the boil. Season with a little salt, reduce the heat and simmer for 10–15 minutes.

3 Meanwhile, cut the pak choi diagonally into wide strips and blanch in boiling water to soften them. Drain and refresh under cold running water to prevent them cooking any further. Bring a large pan of water to the boil, then add the fresh noodles. Cook for 5 minutes, then drain well.

4 Divide the noodles among six soup bowls, lay some of the pak choi and sliced duck over them, and then ladle over generous amounts of the simmering broth. Garnish with the spring onions, chillies and herbs, and serve immediately.

COOK'S TIP
If you can't find fresh egg noodles, substitute dried egg noodles instead. Soak the dried noodles in lukewarm water for 20 minutes, then cook, one portion at a time, in a sieve (strainer) lowered into the boiling water. Use a chopstick to untangle them as they soften. Ready-cooked egg noodles are also available in supermarkets.

Energy 337kcal/1411kJ; Protein 12.1g; Carbohydrate 62.5g, of which sugars 1.1g; Fat 3.3g, of which saturates 0.8g, of which polyunsaturates 0.9g; Cholesterol 41mg; Calcium 66mg; Fibre 0.7g; Sodium 269mg.

CORN FRITTERS ★

THESE LOW-FAT FRITTERS, PACKED WITH CRUNCHY CORN, FRESH CORIANDER AND CHILLI AND ACCOMPANIED WITH DELICIOUS SWEET CHILLI SAUCE, ARE EASY TO PREPARE AND VERY POPULAR.

MAKES TWELVE

INGREDIENTS

3 corn cobs, total weight
  about 250g/9oz
1 garlic clove, crushed
small bunch fresh coriander
  (cilantro), chopped
1 small fresh red or green chilli,
  seeded and finely chopped
1 spring onion (scallion),
  finely chopped
15ml/1 tbsp soy sauce
75g/3oz/¾ cup rice flour or plain
  (all-purpose) flour
2 eggs, lightly beaten
60ml/4 tbsp water
spray oil, for shallow frying
salt and ground black pepper
sweet chilli sauce,
  to serve

1 Using a sharp knife, slice the kernels from the corn cobs and place them in a large bowl. Add the crushed garlic, chopped coriander, chopped and seeded red or green chilli, chopped spring onion, soy sauce, flour, beaten eggs and water and mix well. Season with salt and pepper to taste and mix again. The mixture should be firm enough to hold its shape, but not stiff.

2 Spray a little oil into a large non-stick frying pan. Add spoonfuls of the corn mixture, gently spreading each one out to make a roundish fritter. Cook for 1–2 minutes on each side until golden-brown and cooked through.

3 Drain on kitchen paper and keep hot while frying more fritters in the same way. Serve hot with sweet chilli sauce.

Energy 49kcal/208kJ; Protein 2.3g; Carbohydrate 7.5g, of which sugars 0.6g; Fat 1.3g, of which saturates 0.3g, of which polyunsaturates 0.2g; Cholesterol 32mg; Calcium 21mg; Fibre 0.6g; Sodium 102mg.

CRISPY MIXED VEGETABLE SAMOSAS ★

SURPRISINGLY LOW IN FAT, SAMOSAS ARE SOLD BY STREET VENDORS THROUGHOUT THE EAST. BAKING THE SAMOSAS HELPS KEEP THE FAT CONTENT TO A MINIMUM.

MAKES ABOUT TWENTY

INGREDIENTS
  1 packet 25cm/10in square spring
    roll wrappers, thawed if frozen
  30ml/2 tbsp plain (all-purpose) flour,
    mixed to a paste with water
  about 15ml/1 tbsp sunflower oil
  coriander (cilantro) leaves, to garnish
  cucumber, carrot and celery, cut into
    matchsticks, to serve (optional)
For the filling
  15ml/1 tbsp sunflower oil
  1 small onion, finely chopped
  1cm/$\frac{1}{2}$in piece fresh root ginger,
    peeled and chopped
  1 garlic clove, crushed
  2.5ml/$\frac{1}{2}$ tsp chilli powder
  1 large potato, about 225g/8oz,
    cooked until just tender and
    fincly diced
  50g/2oz/$\frac{1}{2}$ cup cauliflower florets,
    lightly cooked, finely chopped
  50g/2oz/$\frac{1}{2}$ cup frozen peas, thawed
  5–10ml/1–2 tsp garam masala
  15ml/1 tbsp chopped fresh coriander
    (cilantro) leaves and stems
  squeeze of lemon juice
  salt

1 Heat the oil in a large wok and fry the onion, ginger and garlic for 5 minutes until the onion has softened. Add the chilli powder, cook for 1 minute, then stir in the potato, cauliflower and peas. Sprinkle with garam masala and set aside to cool. Stir in the chopped coriander, lemon juice and salt.

2 Preheat the oven to 200°C/400°F/ Gas 6. Cut the spring roll wrappers into three strips (or two for larger samosas). Brush the edges with a little flour paste. Place a small spoonful of filling about 2cm/$\frac{3}{4}$in in from the edge of one strip.

3 Fold one corner over the filling to make a triangle and continue this folding until the entire strip has been used and a triangular pastry has been formed. Seal any open edges with flour and water paste, adding more water if the paste is thick.

4 Place the samosas on a non-stick baking sheet and brush with oil. Bake for about 10 minutes, until crisp. Serve hot garnished with coriander leaves and accompanied by cucumber, carrot and celery matchsticks, if you like.

COOK'S TIP
Filo pastry can be used instead of spring roll wrappers. Cut the pastry into 8.5cm/ 3in wide strips.

Energy 44kcal/186kJ; Protein 1.2g; Carbohydrate 8.3g, of which sugars 0.6g; Fat 0.9g, of which saturates 0.1g, of which polyunsaturates 0.5g; Cholesterol 0mg; Calcium 17mg; Fibre 0.6g; Sodium 2mg.

TUNG TONG ★

POPULARLY CALLED "GOLD BAGS", THESE CRISP PASTRY PURSES HAVE A CORIANDER-FLAVOURED FILLING BASED ON WATER CHESTNUTS AND CORN. THEY ARE THE PERFECT VEGETARIAN SNACK.

MAKES EIGHTEEN

INGREDIENTS
  18 spring roll wrappers, about
    8cm/3¼ in square, thawed
    if frozen
  plum sauce, to serve
  1 egg white
  5ml/1 tsp sunflower oil
For the filling
  4 baby corn cobs
  130g/4½oz can water chestnuts,
    drained and chopped
  1 shallot, coarsely chopped
  1 egg, separated
  30ml/2 tbsp cornflour (cornstarch)
  60ml/4 tbsp water
  small bunch fresh coriander
    (cilantro), chopped
  salt and ground black pepper

1 Make the filling. Place the baby corn, water chestnuts, shallot and egg yolk in a food processor or blender. Process to a coarse paste.

2 Place the egg white in a cup, add the sunflower oil and 5ml/1 tsp water, and whisk it lightly with a fork.

3 Preheat the oven to 180°C/350°F/ Gas 4. Put the cornflour in a small pan and stir in the water until smooth. Add the corn mixture and chopped coriander and season with salt and pepper to taste. Cook over a low heat, stirring constantly, until the mixture boils and thickens.

4 Leave the filling for the pastry purses to cool slightly. Prepare a non-stick baking sheet or line a baking sheet with baking parchment.

5 Place 5ml/1 tsp in the centre of a spring roll wrapper. Brush the edges lightly with the beaten egg white, then gather up the points and press them firmly together to make a pouch or bag.

6 Repeat with remaining wrappers and filling. Brush each pouch generously with the egg white, and place on the baking sheet. Bake for 12–15 minutes, until golden brown. Serve hot, with the plum sauce.

VARIATION
Rice paper wrappers can be used in place of spring roll wrappers if you are following a wheatfree diet. Simply reconstitute the wrappers by brushing them on both sides with warm water to soften them immediately before you use them.

Energy 36kcal/151kJ; Protein 1.5g; Carbohydrate 6.4g, of which sugars 0.4g; Fat 0.7g, of which saturates 0.1g, of which polyunsaturates 0.2g; Cholesterol 11mg; Calcium 17mg; Fibre 0.5g; Sodium 73mg.

THAI TEMPEH CAKES WITH SWEET CHILLI ★

MADE FROM SOYA BEANS, TEMPEH IS SIMILAR TO TOFU BUT HAS A NUTTIER TASTE. HERE, IT IS COMBINED WITH A FRAGRANT BLEND OF LEMON GRASS, CORIANDER AND GINGER.

MAKES EIGHT

INGREDIENTS
    1 lemon grass stalk, outer leaves
        removed and inside finely chopped
    2 garlic cloves, chopped
    2 spring onions (scallions),
        finely chopped
    2 shallots, finely chopped
    2 fresh red chillies, seeded and
        finely chopped
    2.5cm/1in piece fresh root ginger,
        finely chopped
    60ml/4 tbsp chopped fresh coriander
        (cilantro), plus extra to garnish
    250g/9oz/2¼ cups tempeh, thawed if
        frozen, sliced
    15ml/1 tbsp fresh lime juice
    5ml/1 tsp granulated sugar
    45ml/3 tbsp plain (all-purpose) flour
    1 large (US extra large) egg,
        lightly beaten
    salt and ground black pepper
    spray vegetable oil, for frying
For the dipping sauce
    45ml/3 tbsp mirin (see Cook's Tip)
    45ml/3 tbsp white wine vinegar
    2 spring onions (scallions),
        thinly sliced
    15ml/1 tbsp granulated sugar
    2 fresh red chillies, seeded and
        finely chopped
    30ml/2 tbsp chopped fresh
        coriander (cilantro)
    large pinch of salt

1 Make the dipping sauce. Mix together the mirin, vinegar, spring onions, sugar, chillies, coriander and salt in a small bowl. Cover with clear film (plastic wrap) and set aside until ready to serve.

COOK'S TIP
Mirin is a sweet rice wine from Japan. It has quite a delicate flavour and is used for cooking. Rice wine for drinking, called sake, is rather more expensive. Both mirin and sake are available from Asian food stores. If you cannot locate mirin, dry sherry can be used instead, although the results will not be quite the same.

2 Place the lemon grass, garlic, spring onions, shallots, chillies, ginger and coriander in a food processor or blender, then process to a coarse paste. Add the tempeh, lime juice and sugar and process until combined. Add the flour and egg, with salt and pepper to taste. Process again until the mixture forms a coarse, sticky paste.

3 Scrape the paste into a bowl. Take one-eighth of the mixture at a time and form it into rounds with your hands.

4 Spray a little oil in a non-stick frying pan. Fry the cakes for 5–6 minutes, turning once, until golden. Drain on kitchen paper. Transfer to a platter, garnish and serve with the sauce.

Energy 77kcal/322kJ; Protein 4.6g; Carbohydrate 8.4g, of which sugars 3.8g; Fat 2.3g, of which saturates 0.4g, of which polyunsaturates 0.8g; Cholesterol 24mg; Calcium 204mg; Fibre 1.1g; Sodium 16mg.

PAN-STEAMED MUSSELS WITH CHILLI ★

LIKE SO MANY THAI DISHES, THIS IS VERY EASY TO PREPARE AND VERY LOW IN FAT. THE LEMON GRASS AND KAFFIR LIME LEAVES ADD A REFRESHING TANG TO THE MUSSELS.

SERVES SIX

INGREDIENTS

500g/1¼lb fresh mussels
1 lemon grass stalk, finely chopped
2 shallots, chopped
2 kaffir lime leaves, coarsely torn
1 fresh red chilli, sliced
15ml/1 tbsp Thai fish sauce
30ml/2 tbsp fresh lime juice
thinly sliced spring onions (scallions)
   and coriander (cilantro) leaves,
   to garnish

1 Clean the mussels by pulling off the beards, scrubbing the shells well and removing any barnacles. Discard any mussels that are broken or which do not close when tapped sharply.

2 Place the mussels in a large, heavy pan and add the lemon grass, shallots, kaffir lime leaves, chilli, fish sauce and lime juice. Mix well. Cover the pan tightly and steam the mussels over a high heat, shaking the pan occasionally, for 5–7 minutes, until the shells have opened.

3 Using a slotted spoon, transfer the cooked mussels to a warmed serving dish or individual bowls. Discard any mussels that have failed to open.

4 Garnish the mussels with the thinly sliced spring onions and coriander leaves. Serve immediately.

Energy 26kcal/112kJ; Protein 4.5g; Carbohydrate 1g, of which sugars 0.8g; Fat 0.5g, of which saturates 0.1g, of which polyunsaturates 0.2g; Cholesterol 10mg; Calcium 52mg; Fibre 0.1g; Sodium 231mg.

GRILLED PRAWNS <u>WITH</u> LEMON GRASS ★

NEXT TO THE FISH STALL IN EVERY MARKET THERE IS BOUND TO BE SOMEONE COOKING UP FRAGRANT, CITRUS-SCENTED SNACKS FOR YOU TO EAT AS YOU WANDER AROUND THE MARKET.

SERVES FOUR

INGREDIENTS

    16 king prawns (jumbo shrimp),
      cleaned, with shells intact
    120ml/4fl oz/½ cup *nuoc mam*
    30ml/2 tbsp sugar
    15ml/1 tbsp sunflower oil
    3 lemon grass stalks, trimmed and
      finely chopped

1 Using a small sharp knife, carefully slice open each king prawn shell along the back and pull out the black vein, using the point of the knife. Try to keep the rest of the shell intact.

2 Place the deveined prawns in a shallow dish and set aside.

3 Put the *nuoc mam* in a small bowl with the sugar, and beat together until the sugar has dissolved completely. Add the oil and lemon grass and mix well.

COOK'S TIP
Big, juicy king prawns are best for this recipe, but you can use smaller ones if the large king prawns are not available.

4 Pour the marinade over the prawns, using your fingers to rub it all over the prawns and inside the shells too. Cover the dish with clear film (plastic wrap) and chill for at least 4 hours.

5 Cook the prawns on a barbecue or under a conventional grill (broiler) for 2–3 minutes each side. Serve with little bowls of water for rinsing sticky fingers.

Energy 97kcal/409kJ; Protein 9.2g; Carbohydrate 8.8g, of which sugars 8.7g; Fat 3.1g, of which saturates 0.4g, of which polyunsaturates 1.8g; Cholesterol 98mg; Calcium 46mg; Fibre 0g; Sodium 897mg.

FIRECRACKERS ★

IT'S EASY TO SEE HOW THESE PASTRY-WRAPPED PRAWN SNACKS GOT THEIR NAME (KRATHAK IN THAI)
SINCE AS WELL AS RESEMBLING FIREWORKS, THEIR CONTENTS EXPLODE WITH FLAVOUR.

MAKES SIXTEEN

INGREDIENTS
 16 large, raw king prawns (jumbo
  shrimp), heads and shells removed
  but tails left on
 5ml/1 tsp red curry paste
 15ml/1 tbsp Thai fish sauce
 16 small wonton wrappers, about
  8cm/3¼in square, thawed if frozen
 16 fine egg noodles, soaked
  (see Cook's Tip)
 1 egg white
 5ml/1 tsp sunflower oil

1 Place the prawns on their sides and cut two slits through the underbelly of each, one about 1cm/½in from the head end and the other about 1cm/½in from the first cut, cutting across the prawn. This will prevent the prawns from curling when they are cooked.

COOK'S TIP
Soak the fine egg noodles used as ties for the prawn rolls in a bowl of boiling water for 2–3 minutes, until softened, then drain, refresh under cold running water and drain well again.

2 Mix the curry paste with the fish sauce in a shallow dish. Add the prawns and turn them in the mixture until they are well coated. Cover and leave to marinate for 10 minutes.

3 Place a wonton wrapper on the work surface at an angle so that it forms a diamond shape, then fold the top corner over so that the point is in the centre. Place a prawn, slits down, on the wrapper, with the tail projecting from the folded end, then fold the bottom corner over the other end of the prawn.

4 Fold each side of the wrapper over in turn to make a tightly folded roll. Tie a noodle in a bow around the roll and set it aside. Repeat with the remaining prawns and wrappers.

5 Preheat the oven to 240°C/475°F/ Gas 9. Prepare a non-stick baking sheet or line a baking sheet with baking parchment. Lightly whisk the egg white with the oil and 5ml/1 tsp water. Brush the wrapped prawns generously with egg white, so they are well moistened, and place on the baking sheet. Bake for 5–6 minutes, until crisp and lightly browned.

Energy 37kcal/155kJ; Protein 2.1g; Carbohydrate 6g, of which sugars 0.2g; Fat 0.6g, of which saturates 0.1g, of which polyunsaturates 0.2g; Cholesterol 13mg; Calcium 13mg; Fibre 0.2g; Sodium 88mg.

CRISPY SPRING ROLLS ★

IT IS SAID THAT THESE FAMOUS SNACKS WERE TRADITIONALLY SERVED WITH TEA WHEN VISITORS CAME TO CALL AFTER THE NEW YEAR. AS THIS WAS SPRINGTIME, THEY CAME TO BE KNOWN AS SPRING ROLLS.

MAKES TWELVE

INGREDIENTS
  12 spring roll wrappers, thawed
    if frozen
  30ml/2 tbsp plain (all-purpose) flour
    mixed to a paste with water
For the filling
  6 Chinese dried mushrooms,
    soaked for 30 minutes in
    warm water
  150g/5oz fresh firm tofu
  15ml/1 tbsp sunflower oil
  225g/8oz finely minced (ground)
    lean pork
  225g/8oz peeled cooked prawns
    (shrimp), roughly chopped
  2.5ml/½ tsp cornflour (cornstarch),
    mixed to a paste with 15ml/1 tbsp
    light soy sauce
  75g/3oz each shredded bamboo shoot
    or grated carrot, sliced water
    chestnuts and beansprouts
  6 spring onions (scallions) or 1 young
    leek, finely chopped
  2.5ml/½ tsp sesame oil
For the dipping sauce
  100ml/3½ fl oz/scant ½ cup
    light soy sauce
  15ml/1 tbsp chilli sauce or finely
    chopped fresh red chilli
  a little sesame oil
  rice vinegar, to taste

1 Make the filling. Drain the mushrooms. Cut off and discard the stems and slice the caps finely. Cut the tofu into slices of a similar size.

2 Heat the oil in a wok and stir-fry the pork for 2–3 minutes or until the colour changes. Add the prawns, cornflour paste and bamboo shoot or carrot. Stir in the water chestnuts.

COOK'S TIP
Thaw frozen spring roll wrappers at room temperature. Separate with a metal spatula. Cover with a damp cloth until needed.

3 Increase the heat, add the beansprouts and finely chopped spring onions or leek and toss the mixture for 1 minute. Stir in the dried Chinese mushrooms and tofu.

4 Off the heat, season the mixture to taste, and then stir in the sesame oil. Cool quickly on a large platter.

5 Separate the spring roll wrappers (see Cook's Tip). Place a wrapper on the work surface with one corner nearest you. Spoon some of the filling near the centre of the wrapper and fold the nearest corner over the filling. Smear a little of the flour paste on the free sides, turn the sides to the middle and roll up. Repeat this procedure with the remaining wrappers and filling.

6 Preheat the oven to 200°C/400°F/ Gas 6. Prepare a non-stick baking sheet or line a baking sheet with non-stick baking parchment. Lightly whisk the egg white with the oil and 5ml/1 tsp water. Generously brush the spring rolls with egg white, so they are moistened all over, and place on the baking sheet. Bake for about 20 minutes, until crisp and golden.

Energy 83kcal/349kJ; Protein 9.5g; Carbohydrate 7.9g, of which sugars 1.4g; Fat 1.7g, of which saturates 0.4g, of which polyunsaturates 0.5g; Cholesterol 48mg; Calcium 97mg; Fibre 0.5g; Sodium 645mg.

FISH AND SHELLFISH

Fish is a main source of protein in the Thai diet, which is hardly surprising considering the vast lengths of coastline. Enjoy the health benefits of omega-3 fatty acids and impress your guests with Trout with Tamarind and Chilli Sauce, Jungle Fish Cooked in Banana Leaves, or Northern Fish Curry.

FISH IN COCONUT CUSTARD ★★

THIS IS A KHMER CLASSIC. RICH AND SUMPTUOUS, AMOK TREY CROPS UP ALL OVER CAMBODIA. IN PHNOM PENH, THERE ARE RESTAURANTS THAT SPECIALIZE IN IT. THE FISH IS STEAMED IN A CUSTARD, MADE WITH COCONUT MILK AND FLAVOURED WITH THE CAMBODIAN HERBAL PASTE, KROEUNG.

SERVES FOUR

INGREDIENTS
  2 x 400ml/14oz cans reduced-fat
    coconut milk
  3 eggs
  80ml/3fl oz *kroeung*
  15ml/1 tbsp *tuk trey*
  10ml/2 tsp palm sugar or honey
  1 kg/2¼lb fresh, skinned white fish
    fillets, cut into 8 pieces
  1 small bunch chopped fresh
    coriander (cilantro), plus a few
    whole sprigs, to garnish
  jasmine rice or crusty bread and
    salad, to serve

VARIATION
This dish can also be cooked in the oven in a bain marie. Cook at 160°C/325°F/Gas 3 for about 50 minutes.

1 Half fill a wok or large pan with water. Set a bamboo or stainless-steel steamer over it and put the lid on. Bring the water to the boil.

2 In a bowl, beat the reduced-fat coconut milk with the eggs, *kroeung*, *tuk trey* and sugar or honey, until everything is well blended and the sugar has dissolved.

3 Place the fish fillets in a heatproof dish that will fit in the steamer. Pour the coconut mixture over the fish and place the dish in the steamer. Put the lid back on the steamer and reduce the heat so that the custard won't curdle. Steam over gently simmering water until the fish is cooked. Garnish with coriander and serve immediately with jasmine rice or crusty bread and salad.

Energy 314kcal/1324kJ; Protein 51.1g; Carbohydrate 13.6g, of which sugars 13.6g; Fat 6.5g, of which saturates 1.8g, of which polyunsaturates 1.2g; Cholesterol 258mg; Calcium 102mg; Fibre 0g; Sodium 423mg.

CATFISH COOKED IN A CLAY POT ★

WONDERFULLY EASY AND TASTY, THIS SOUTHERN-STYLE VIETNAMESE AND CAMBODIAN DISH IS A CLASSIC. IN THE SOUTH OF VIETNAM, CLAY POTS ARE REGULARLY USED FOR COOKING AND THEY ENHANCE BOTH THE LOOK AND TASTE OF THIS TRADITIONAL DISH.

SERVES FOUR

INGREDIENTS
  30ml/2 tbsp sugar
  15ml/1 tbsp sunflower oil
  2 garlic cloves, crushed
  45ml/3 tbsp *nuoc mam*
  350g/12oz catfish fillets, cut
    diagonally into 2 or 3 pieces
  4 spring onions (scallions), cut
    into bitesize pieces
  ground black pepper
  chopped fresh coriander (cilantro),
    to garnish
  fresh bread, to serve

2 Stir the *nuoc mam* into the caramel mixture and add 120ml/4fl oz/½ cup boiling water, then toss in the catfish pieces, making sure they are well coated with the sauce. Cover the pot, reduce the heat and simmer for about 5 minutes.

3 Remove the lid, season with ground black pepper and gently stir in the spring onions. Simmer for a further 3–4 minutes to thicken the sauce, garnish with fresh coriander, and serve immediately straight from the pot with chunks of fresh bread.

1 Place the sugar in a clay pot or heavy pan, and add 15ml/1 tbsp water to wet it. Heat the sugar until it begins to turn golden brown, then add the oil and crushed garlic.

Energy 128kcal/537kJ; Protein 16.4g; Carbohydrate 8.3g, of which sugars 8.3g; Fat 3.4g, of which saturates 0.4g, of which polyunsaturates 2g; Cholesterol 40mg; Calcium 18mg; Fibre 0.2g; Sodium 54mg.

THAI-STYLE TROUT ★★

THE COMBINATION OF CLASSIC THAI AROMATIC INGREDIENTS GIVES THIS SIMPLE DISH A FABULOUS
FLAVOUR. SERVE WITH PLENTY OF STEAMED THAI FRAGRANT RICE TO SOAK UP THE DELICIOUS SAUCE.

SERVES FOUR

INGREDIENTS
200g/7oz spinach leaves
1 lemon grass stalk, finely chopped
2.5cm/1in piece fresh root ginger,
  peeled and finely grated
2 garlic cloves, crushed
200ml/7fl oz/scant 1 cup reduced-fat
  coconut milk
30ml/2 tbsp lime juice
15ml/1 tbsp soft light brown sugar
4 trout fillets, each about 200g/7oz
salt and ground black pepper
steamed Thai fragrant rice, to serve

COOK'S TIP
To steam Thai fragrant rice, cook it in
a pan of salted boiling water for three-
quarters of the time noted on the packet.
Transfer it to a colander lined with muslin
or cheesecloth and steam over simmering
water for 5–10 minutes until just tender.

1 Preheat the oven to 200°C/400°F/
Gas 6. Place the spinach in a pan, with
just the water that adheres to the leaves
after washing. Cover with a lid and cook
gently for 3–4 minutes until the leaves
have just wilted. Drain the spinach in a
colander and press it with the back of
a spoon to remove any excess moisture.

2 Transfer the spinach to a mixing bowl
and stir in the chopped lemon grass,
grated ginger and garlic.

3 Combine the coconut milk, lime juice,
sugar and seasoning in a jug (pitcher).
Place the trout fillets side by side in
a shallow baking dish and pour the
coconut milk mixture over.

4 Bake the trout for 20–25 minutes
until cooked. Place on individual serving
plates, on top of the steamed Thai
fragrant rice. Toss the spinach mixture
in the juices remaining in the dish,
spoon on top of the fish and serve.

Energy 266kcal/1119kJ; Protein 40.5g; Carbohydrate 7.9g, of which sugars 7.7g; Fat 8.3g, of which saturates 0.2g, of which polyunsaturates 0.3g; Cholesterol 0mg; Calcium 140mg; Fibre 1.7g; Sodium 177mg.

TROUT WITH TAMARIND AND CHILLI SAUCE ★★

SOMETIMES TROUT CAN TASTE RATHER BLAND, BUT THIS SPICY SAUCE REALLY GIVES IT A ZING.
IF YOU LIKE YOUR FOOD VERY SPICY, ADD AN EXTRA CHILLI.

SERVES FOUR

INGREDIENTS
　　4 trout, cleaned
　　6 spring onions (scallions), sliced
　　60ml/4 tbsp soy sauce
　　spray sunflower oil, for frying
　　30ml/2 tbsp chopped fresh coriander
　　　(cilantro) and strips of fresh red
　　　chilli, to garnish
For the sauce
　　50g/2oz tamarind pulp
　　105ml/7 tbsp boiling water
　　2 shallots, coarsely chopped
　　1 fresh red chilli, seeded and chopped
　　1cm/½in piece fresh root ginger,
　　　peeled and chopped
　　5ml/1 tsp soft light brown sugar
　　45ml/3 tbsp Thai fish sauce

3 Make the sauce. Put the tamarind pulp in a small bowl and pour on the boiling water. Mash well with a fork until softened. Tip the tamarind mixture into a food processor or blender, and add the shallots, fresh chilli, ginger, sugar and fish sauce. Process to a coarse pulp. Scrape into a bowl.

4 Spray a large frying pan with oil. Heat and cook the trout, one at a time if necessary, for about 5 minutes on each side, until the skin is crisp and browned and the flesh cooked. Put on warmed plates and spoon over some of the sauce. Sprinkle with the coriander and chilli and serve with the remaining sauce.

1 Slash the trout diagonally four or five times on each side. Place them in a shallow dish that is large enough to hold them all in a single layer.

2 Fill the cavities with spring onions and douse each fish with soy sauce. Carefully turn the fish over to coat both sides with the sauce. Sprinkle any remaining spring onions over the top.

Energy 215kcal/904kJ; Protein 35.4g; Carbohydrate 3.2g, of which sugars 2.7g; Fat 6.8g, of which saturates 1.6g, of which polyunsaturates 2.3g; Cholesterol 144mg; Calcium 60mg; Fibre 0.2g; Sodium 932mg.

NORTHERN FISH CURRY ★★

THIS IS A THIN, SOUPY CURRY WITH WONDERFULLY STRONG FLAVOURS. SERVE IT IN BOWLS WITH LOTS OF FRESHLY STEAMED STICKY RICE TO ABSORB THE DELICIOUS JUICES.

SERVES FOUR

INGREDIENTS

   350g/12oz salmon fillet
   500ml/17fl oz/2¼ cups
     vegetable stock
   4 shallots, finely chopped
   2 garlic cloves, finely chopped
   2.5cm/1in piece fresh galangal,
     finely chopped
   1 lemon grass stalk, finely chopped
   2.5ml/½ tsp dried chilli flakes
   15ml/1 tbsp Thai fish sauce
   5ml/1 tsp palm sugar or light
     muscovado (brown) sugar

1 Place the salmon in the freezer for 30–40 minutes to firm up the flesh slightly. Remove and discard the skin, then use a sharp knife to cut the fish into 2.5cm/1in cubes, removing any stray bones with your fingers or with tweezers as you do so.

2 Pour the stock into a large, heavy pan and bring it to the boil over a medium heat. Add the shallots, garlic, galangal, lemon grass, chilli flakes, fish sauce and sugar. Bring back to the boil, stir well, then reduce the heat and simmer gently for 15 minutes.

3 Add the fish, bring back to the boil, then turn off the heat. Leave the curry to stand for 10–15 minutes until the fish is cooked through, then serve.

Energy 172kcal/717kJ; Protein 18.2g; Carbohydrate 3.2g, of which sugars 2.5g; Fat 9.7g, of which saturates 1.7g, of which polyunsaturates 2.7g; Cholesterol 44mg; Calcium 24mg; Fibre 0.3g; Sodium 307mg.

ESCABECHE ★

THIS PICKLED FISH DISH IS EATEN WHEREVER THERE ARE — OR HAVE BEEN — SPANISH SETTLERS.
IT IS ESPECIALLY POPULAR IN THE PHILIPPINES WHERE IT IS SERVED WITH BOILED OR STEAMED RICE.

SERVES SIX

INGREDIENTS
   675–900g/1½–2lb white fish fillets,
      such as sole or plaice
   45–60ml/3–4 tbsp seasoned flour
   sunflower oil, for shallow frying
For the sauce
   2.5cm/1in piece fresh root ginger,
      peeled and thinly sliced
   2–3 garlic cloves, crushed
   1 onion, cut into thin rings
   15ml/1 tbsp sunflower oil
   ½ large green (bell) pepper,
      seeded and cut in small
      neat squares
   ½ large red (bell) pepper, seeded
      and cut in small neat squares
   1 carrot, cut into matchsticks
   25ml/1½ tbsp cornflour (cornstarch)
   450ml/¾ pint/scant 2 cups water
   45–60ml/3–4 tbsp herb or
      cider vinegar
   15ml/1 tbsp light soft brown sugar
   5–10ml/1–2 tsp Thai fish sauce
   salt and ground black pepper
   1 small chilli, seeded and sliced
      and spring onions (scallions), finely
      shredded, to garnish (optional)
   boiled rice, to serve

1 Wipe the fish fillets and leave them whole, or cut into serving portions, if you like. Pat dry on kitchen paper then dust lightly with seasoned flour.

2 Heat oil for shallow frying in a frying pan and fry the fish in batches until golden and almost cooked. Transfer to an ovenproof dish and keep warm.

3 Make the sauce in a wok or large frying pan. Fry the ginger, garlic and onion in the oil for 5 minutes or until the onion is softened but not browned.

4 Add the pepper squares and carrot strips and stir-fry for 1 minute.

5 Put the cornflour in a small bowl and add a little of the water to make a paste. Stir in the remaining water, the vinegar and the sugar. Pour the cornflour mixture over the vegetables in the wok and stir until the sauce boils and thickens a little. Season with fish sauce and salt and pepper if needed.

6 Add the fish to the sauce and reheat briefly without stirring. Transfer to a warmed serving platter and garnish with chilli and spring onions, if liked. Serve with boiled rice.

COOK'S TIP
Red snapper or small sea bass could be used for this recipe, in which case ask your fishmonger to cut them into fillets.

JUNGLE FISH COOKED <u>IN</u> BANANA LEAVES ★

STEAMING FRESHWATER FISH IN BANANA LEAVES OVER HOT CHARCOAL IS A TRADITIONAL METHOD OF COOKING IN THE JUNGLE. BANANA LEAVES ARE LARGE AND TOUGH, AND SERVE AS BASIC COOKING VESSELS AND WRAPPERS FOR ALL SORTS OF FISH AND MEAT.

SERVES FOUR

INGREDIENTS
350g/12oz freshwater fish fillets,
  such as trout, cut into
  bitesize chunks
6 banana leaves (see Cook's Tip)
spray sunflower vegetable oil
sticky rice, noodles or salad, to serve
For the marinade
2 shallots
5cm/2in turmeric root, peeled
  and grated
2 spring onions (scallions),
  finely sliced
2 garlic cloves, crushed
1–2 green Thai chillies, seeded
  and finely chopped
15ml/1 tbsp *nuoc mam*
2.5ml/½ tsp raw cane sugar
salt and ground black pepper

1 To make the marinade, grate the shallots into a bowl, then combine with the other marinade ingredients, Season with salt and pepper. Toss the chunks of fish in the marinade, then cover and chill for 6 hours, or overnight.

VARIATION
This dish can be made with any of the catfish or carp family, or even tilapia.

2 Prepare a barbecue. Place one of the banana leaves on a flat surface and spray it with oil. Place the marinated fish on the banana leaf, spreading it out evenly, then fold over the sides to form an envelope. Place this envelope, fold side down, on top of another leaf and fold that one in the same manner. Repeat with the remaining leaves until they are all used up.

3 Secure the last layer of banana leaf with a piece of bendy wire. Place the banana leaf packet on the barbecue. Cook for about 20 minutes, turning it over from time to time to make sure it is cooked on both sides – the outer leaves will burn. Carefully untie the wire (it will be hot) and unravel the packet. Check that the fish is cooked and serve with sticky rice, noodles or salad.

COOK'S TIP
Banana leaves are available in some African and Asian stores and markets. If you can't find them, wrap the fish in vine leaves that have been soaked in cold water, or large flexible cabbage leaves. You can also use foil.

Energy 84kcal/352kJ; Protein 16.3g; Carbohydrate 1.5g, of which sugars 1.1g; Fat 1.4g, of which saturates 0.2g, of which polyunsaturates 0.8g; Cholesterol 40mg; Calcium 12mg; Fibre 0.2g; Sodium 320mg.

STEAMED FISH <u>WITH</u> CHILLI SAUCE ★

STEAMING IS ONE OF THE HEALTHIEST METHODS OF COOKING FISH. BY LEAVING THE FISH WHOLE AND ON THE BONE, MAXIMUM FLAVOUR IS RETAINED AND THE FLESH REMAINS BEAUTIFULLY MOIST. THE BANANA LEAF IS BOTH AUTHENTIC AND ATTRACTIVE, BUT YOU CAN USE BAKING PARCHMENT.

SERVES FOUR

INGREDIENTS
  1 large or 2 medium firm fish such as sea bass or grouper, scaled and cleaned
  30ml/2 tbsp rice wine
  3 fresh red chillies, seeded and thinly sliced
  2 garlic cloves, finely chopped
  2cm/¾in piece fresh root ginger, peeled and finely shredded
  2 lemon grass stalks, crushed and finely chopped
  2 spring onions (scallions), chopped
  30ml/2 tbsp Thai fish sauce
  juice of 1 lime
  1 fresh banana leaf
For the chilli sauce
  10 fresh red chillies, seeded and chopped
  4 garlic cloves, chopped
  60ml/4 tbsp Thai fish sauce
  15ml/1 tbsp granulated sugar
  75ml/5 tbsp fresh lime juice

1 Thoroughly rinse the fish under cold running water. Pat it dry with kitchen paper. With a sharp knife, slash the skin of the fish a few times on both sides.

2 Mix together the rice wine, chillies, garlic, shredded ginger, lemon grass and spring onions in a non-metallic bowl. Add the fish sauce and lime juice and mix to a paste. Place the fish on the banana leaf and spread the spice paste evenly over it, rubbing it in well where the skin has been slashed.

3 Put a rack or a small upturned plate in the base of a wok. Pour in boiling water to a depth of 5cm/2in. Lift the banana leaf, together with the fish, and place it on the rack or plate. Cover with a lid and steam for 10–15 minutes, or until the fish is cooked.

4 Meanwhile, make the sauce. Place all the ingredients in a food processor and process until smooth. If the mixture seems to be too thick, add a little cold water. Scrape into a serving bowl.

5 Serve the fish hot, on the banana leaf if you like, with the sweet chilli sauce to spoon over the top.

Energy 147kcal/619kJ; Protein 28.4g; Carbohydrate 5.5g, of which sugars 5.3g; Fat 1.3g, of which saturates 0.2g, of which polyunsaturates 0.5g; Cholesterol 69mg; Calcium 56mg; Fibre 1g; Sodium 89.8mg.

CURRIED SEAFOOD WITH COCONUT MILK ★

THIS CURRY IS BASED ON A THAI CLASSIC. THE LOVELY GREEN COLOUR IS IMPARTED BY THE FINELY CHOPPED CHILLI AND FRESH HERBS ADDED DURING THE LAST FEW MOMENTS OF COOKING.

SERVES FOUR

INGREDIENTS
225g/8oz small ready-prepared squid
225g/8oz raw tiger prawns
(jumbo shrimp)
400ml/14fl oz/1⅔ cups reduced-fat
coconut milk
2 kaffir lime leaves, finely shredded
30ml/2 tbsp Thai fish sauce
450g/1lb firm white fish fillets,
skinned, boned and cut into chunks
2 fresh green chillies, seeded and
finely chopped
30ml/2 tbsp torn fresh basil or
coriander (cilantro) leaves
squeeze of fresh lime juice
cooked Thai jasmine rice, to serve
For the curry paste
6 spring onions (scallions),
coarsely chopped
4 fresh coriander (cilantro) stems,
coarsely chopped, plus 45ml/3 tbsp
chopped fresh coriander (cilantro)
4 kaffir lime leaves, shredded
8 fresh green chillies, seeded and
coarsely chopped
1 lemon grass stalk,
coarsely chopped
2.5cm/1in piece fresh root ginger,
peeled and coarsely chopped
45ml/3 tbsp chopped fresh basil
5ml/1 tsp sunflower oil

1 Make the curry paste. Put all the ingredients, except the oil, in a food processor and process to a paste. Alternatively, pound together in a mortar with a pestle. Stir in the oil.

2 Rinse the squid and pat dry with kitchen paper. Cut the bodies into rings and halve the tentacles, if necessary.

3 Heat a wok until hot, add the prawns and stir-fry, without any oil, for about 4 minutes, until they turn pink.

4 Remove the prawns from the wok and leave to cool slightly, then peel off the shells, saving a few with shells on for the garnish. Make a slit along the back of each one and remove the black vein.

5 Pour the coconut milk into the wok, then bring to the boil over a medium heat, stirring constantly. Add 30ml/ 2 tbsp of curry paste, the shredded lime leaves and fish sauce and stir well to mix. Reduce the heat to low and simmer gently for about 10 minutes.

6 Add the squid, prawns and chunks of fish and cook for about 2 minutes, until the seafood is tender. Take care not to overcook the squid as it will become tough very quickly.

7 Just before serving, stir in the chillies and the torn basil or coriander leaves. Taste and adjust the flavour with a squeeze of lime juice. Garnish the curry with prawns in their shells, and serve with Thai jasmine rice.

VARIATIONS
• You can use any firm-fleshed white fish for this curry, such as monkfish, cod, haddock or John Dory.
• If you prefer, you could substitute shelled scallops for the squid. Slice them in half horizontally and add them with the prawns (shrimp). As with the squid, be careful not to overcook them.

Energy 211kcal/894kJ; Protein 39.8g; Carbohydrate 5.9g, of which sugars 5.2g; Fat 3.3g, of which saturates 0.7g, of which polyunsaturates 1.2g; Cholesterol 288mg; Calcium 116mg; Fibre 0.6g; Sodium 351mg.

PRAWN AND CAULIFLOWER CURRY ★

THIS IS A BASIC FISHERMAN'S CURRY FROM THE SOUTHERN COAST OF VIETNAM. SIMPLE TO MAKE, IT WOULD USUALLY BE EATEN FROM A COMMUNAL BOWL, OR FROM THE WOK ITSELF, AND SERVED WITH NOODLES, RICE OR CHUNKS OF BAGUETTE TO MOP UP THE DELICIOUSLY FRAGRANT SAUCE.

SERVES FOUR

INGREDIENTS

450g/1lb raw tiger prawns (jumbo shrimp), shelled and cleaned
juice of 1 lime
15ml/1 tbsp sunflower oil
1 red onion, roughly chopped
2 garlic cloves, roughly chopped
2 Thai chillies, seeded and chopped
1 cauliflower, broken into florets
5ml/1 tsp sugar
2 star anise, dry-fried and ground
10ml/2 tsp fenugreek, dry-fried and ground
450ml/¾ pint/2 cups reduced-fat coconut milk
chopped fresh coriander (cilantro) leaves, to garnish
salt and ground black pepper

1 In a bowl, toss the prawns in the lime juice and set aside. Heat a wok or heavy pan and add the oil. Stir in the onion, garlic and chillies. As they brown, add the cauliflower. Stir-fry for 2–3 minutes.

VARIATION
Other popular combinations include prawns with butternut squash or pumpkin.

2 Toss in the sugar and spices. Add the coconut milk, stirring to make sure it is thoroughly combined. Reduce the heat and simmer for 10–15 minutes, or until the liquid has reduced and thickened a little. Add the prawns and lime juice and cook for 1–2 minutes, or until the prawns turn opaque. Season to taste, and sprinkle with coriander. Serve hot.

Energy 157kcal/664kJ; Protein 24.7g; Carbohydrate 10.4g, of which sugars 9.4g; Fat 2.2g, of which saturates 0.6g, of which polyunsaturates 0.7g; Cholesterol 219mg; Calcium 169mg; Fibre 2.7g; Sodium 352mg.

LOBSTER AND CRAB STEAMED IN BEER ★

IN SPITE OF ITS APPEARANCE ON MENUS IN RESTAURANTS THAT SPECIALIZE IN THE COMPLEX AND REFINED IMPERIAL DISHES OF VIETNAM, THIS RECIPE IS VERY EASY TO MAKE. IT MAY BE EXPENSIVE, BUT IT'S A WONDERFUL DISH FOR A SPECIAL OCCASION.

SERVES FOUR TO SIX

INGREDIENTS

- 4 uncooked lobsters, about 450g/1lb each
- 4 uncooked crabs, about 225g/8oz each
- 600ml/1 pint/2½ cups beer
- 4 spring onions (scallions), trimmed and chopped into long pieces
- 4cm/1½in fresh root ginger, peeled and finely sliced
- 2 green or red Thai chillies, seeded and finely sliced
- 3 lemon grass stalks, finely sliced
- 1 bunch fresh dill, fronds chopped
- 1 bunch each fresh basil and coriander (cilantro), stalks removed, leaves chopped
- about 30ml/2 tbsp *nuoc mam*, plus extra for serving
- juice of 1 lemon
- salt and ground black pepper

1 Clean the lobsters and crabs thoroughly and rub them with salt and pepper. Place them in a large steamer and pour the beer into the base.

2 Sprinkle half the spring onions, ginger, chillies, lemon grass and herbs over the lobsters and crabs, and steam for about 10 minutes, or until the lobsters turn red. Lift them on to a warmed serving dish.

VARIATIONS

Prawns (shrimp) and mussels are also delicious cooked this way. Replace the lemon with lime if you like.

3 Add the remaining flavouring ingredients to the beer with the *nuoc mam* and lemon juice. Pour into a dipping bowl and serve immediately with the hot lobsters and crabs, with extra splashes of *nuoc mam*, if you like.

COOK'S TIP

Whether you cook the lobsters and crabs at the same time depends on the number of people you are cooking for and the size of your steamer. However, they don't take long to cook so it is easy to steam them in batches. In the markets and restaurants of Vietnam, you can find crabs that are 60cm/24in in diameter, which may feed several people but require a huge steamer. Depending on the size and availability of the lobsters and crabs, you can make this recipe for as many people as you like, because the quantities are simple to adjust. For those who like their food fiery, splash a little chilli sauce into the beer broth.

Energy 190kcal/801kJ; Protein 35.2g; Carbohydrate 1.5g, of which sugars 1.4g; Fat 4.9g, of which saturates 0.7g, of which polyunsaturates 1.6g; Cholesterol 158mg; Calcium 86mg; Fibre 0.8g; Sodium 589mg.

GREEN PRAWN CURRY ★

GREEN CURRY HAS BECOME A FIRM FAVOURITE IN THE WEST, AND THIS PRAWN DISH IS JUST ONE OF A RANGE OF DELICIOUS GREEN CURRY RECIPES. HOME-MADE GREEN CURRY PASTE HAS THE BEST FLAVOUR, BUT YOU CAN ALSO BUY IT FROM GOOD SUPERMARKETS.

2 Add the prawns, kaffir lime leaves and chopped lemon grass. Fry for 2 minutes, until the prawns are pink.

3 Stir in the coconut milk and bring to a gentle boil. Simmer, stirring for about 5 minutes or until the prawns are tender.

4 Stir in the fish sauce, cucumber batons and whole basil leaves, then top with the green chillies and serve from the pan.

VARIATION
Strips of skinless chicken breast fillet can be used in place of the prawns if you prefer. Add them to the pan in step 2 and fry until browned on all sides.

SERVES SIX

INGREDIENTS
  15ml/1 tbsp sunflower oil
  30ml/2 tbsp green curry paste
  450g/1lb raw king prawns (jumbo shrimp), peeled and deveined
  4 kaffir lime leaves, torn
  1 lemon grass stalk, bruised and chopped
  250ml/8fl oz/1 cup reduced-fat coconut milk
  30ml/2 tbsp Thai fish sauce
  ½ cucumber, seeded and cut into thin batons
  10–15 basil leaves
  4 green chillies, sliced, to garnish

1 Heat the sunflower oil in a wok or large pan until sizzling hot. Add the green curry paste and fry over a gentle heat for several minutes until bubbling and fragrant, stirring the mixture continually with chopsticks.

Energy 92kcal/385kJ; Protein 13.7g; Carbohydrate 2.6g, of which sugars 2.5g; Fat 3g, of which saturates 0.5g, of which polyunsaturates 1.6g; Cholesterol 146mg; Calcium 92mg; Fibre 0.4g; Sodium 191mg.

PRAWNS WITH YELLOW CURRY PASTE ★

FISH AND SHELLFISH, SUCH AS PRAWNS, AND COCONUT MILK WERE MADE FOR EACH OTHER. THIS IS A VERY QUICK RECIPE IF YOU MAKE THE YELLOW CURRY PASTE IN ADVANCE, OR BUY IT READY-MADE. IT KEEPS WELL IN A SCREW-TOP JAR IN THE REFRIGERATOR FOR UP TO FOUR WEEKS.

SERVES SIX

INGREDIENTS

600ml/1 pint/2½ cups reduced-fat
  coconut milk
30ml/2 tbsp yellow curry paste
15ml/1 tbsp Thai fish sauce
2.5ml/½ tsp salt
5ml/1 tsp granulated sugar
450g/1lb raw king prawns (jumbo
  shrimp), peeled and deveined
225g/8oz cherry tomatoes
juice of ½ lime
red (bell) peppers, seeded and
  cut into thin strips, and fresh
  coriander (cilantro) leaves,
  to garnish

1 Put half the coconut milk in a wok or large pan and bring to the boil. Add the yellow curry paste and stir until it disperses. Lower the heat and simmer gently for about 10 minutes.

2 Add the fish sauce, salt, sugar and remaining coconut milk to the sauce. Simmer for 5 minutes more.

3 Add the prawns and cherry tomatoes. Simmer very gently for about 5 minutes until the prawns are pink and tender.

4 Spoon into a serving dish, sprinkle with lime juice and garnish with strips of pepper and coriander.

COOK'S TIPS
• Unused coconut milk can be stored in the refrigerator for 1–2 days, or poured into a freezer container and frozen for up to a month.
• If making your own coconut milk, instead of discarding the spent coconut, it can be reused to make a second batch of coconut milk. However, this will be of a poorer quality and it should only be used to extend a good quality first quantity of milk.
• To make coconut cream, leave newly made coconut milk to stand for 10 minutes. The coconut cream will float to the top – skim it off with a spoon and use in the usual way.

Energy 94kcal/397kJ; Protein 13.8g; Carbohydrate 7g, of which sugars 6.9g; Fat 1.4g, of which saturates 0.4g, of which polyunsaturates 0.5g; Cholesterol 146mg; Calcium 92mg; Fibre 0.4g; Sodium 434mg.

SINIGANG ★

MANY FILIPINOS WOULD CONSIDER THIS SOURED HEALTHY SOUP-LIKE STEW TO BE THEIR NATIONAL DISH. IT IS ALWAYS SERVED WITH NOODLES OR RICE. IN ADDITION, FISH — IN THE FORM OF EITHER PRAWNS OR THIN SLIVERS OF FISH FILLET — IS OFTEN ADDED FOR GOOD MEASURE.

3 Pour the prepared fish stock into a large pan and add the diced mooli. Cook the mooli for 5 minutes, then add the beans and continue to cook for 3–5 minutes more.

SERVES SIX

INGREDIENTS
15ml/1 tbsp tamarind pulp
150ml/¼ pint/⅔ cup warm water
2 tomatoes
115g/4oz spinach or Chinese leaves
  (Chinese cabbage)
115g/4oz peeled cooked large prawns
  (shrimp), thawed if frozen
1.2 litres/2 pints/5 cups prepared
  fish stock (see Cook's Tip)
½ mooli (daikon), peeled and diced
115g/4oz green beans, cut into
  1cm/½in lengths
225g/8oz piece of cod or haddock
  fillet, skinned and cut into strips
Thai fish sauce, to taste
squeeze of lemon juice, to taste
salt and ground black pepper
boiled rice or noodles, to serve

1 Put the tamarind pulp in a bowl and pour over the warm water. Set aside while you peel and chop the tomatoes, discarding the seeds. Strip the spinach or Chinese leaves from the stems and tear into small pieces.

2 Remove the heads and shells from the prawns, leaving the tails intact.

4 Add the fish strips, tomato and spinach. Strain in the tamarind juice and cook for 2 minutes. Stir in the prawns and cook for 1–2 minutes to heat. Season with salt and pepper and add a little fish sauce and lemon juice to taste. Transfer to individual serving bowls and serve immediately, with rice or noodles.

COOK'S TIP
A good fish stock is essential for this dish. Ask your fishmonger for about 675g/1½lb fish bones. Wash them, then place in a large pan with 2 litres/ 3½ pints/8 cups water. Add half a peeled onion, a piece of bruised peeled ginger, and a little salt and pepper. Bring to the boil, skim, then simmer for 20 minutes. Cool slightly, then strain. Freeze unused fish stock.

Energy 52kcal/218kJ, Protein 10.6g; Carbohydrate 1.3g, of which sugars 1.3g; Fat 0.5g, of which saturates 0.1g, of which polyunsaturates 0.2g; Cholesterol 55mg; Calcium 31mg; Fibre 0.6g; Sodium 62mg.

STIR-FRIED BABY SQUID <u>WITH</u> GINGER ★★

THE ABUNDANCE OF FISH AROUND THE GULF OF THAILAND SUSTAINS THRIVING MARKETS FOR THE RESTAURANT AND HOTEL TRADE, AND EVERY MARKET NATURALLY FEATURES STALLS WHERE DELICIOUS, FRESHLY CAUGHT SEAFOOD IS COOKED AND SERVED. THIS RECIPE IS POPULAR AMONG STREET TRADERS.

SERVES TWO

INGREDIENTS

4 ready-prepared baby squid,
  total weight about 250g/9oz
15ml/1 tbsp sunflower oil
2 garlic cloves, finely chopped
30ml/2 tbsp soy sauce
2.5cm/1in piece fresh root ginger,
  peeled and finely chopped
juice of ½ lemon
5ml/1 tsp granulated sugar
2 spring onions (scallions), chopped

VARIATIONS

This dish is often prepared with fresh galangal rather than ginger and works well with most kinds of seafood, including prawns (shrimp) and scallops.

1 Rinse the squid well and pat dry with kitchen paper. Cut the bodies into rings and halve the tentacles, if necessary.

2 Heat the oil in a wok or frying pan and cook the garlic until golden brown, but do not let it burn. Add the squid and stir-fry for 30 seconds over a high heat.

3 Add the soy sauce, ginger, lemon juice, sugar and spring onions. Stir-fry for a further 30 seconds, then serve.

COOK'S TIP

Squid has an undeserved reputation for being rubbery in texture. This is always a result of overcooking it.

Energy 169kcal/709kJ; Protein 20g; Carbohydrate 5.3g, of which sugars 3.6g; Fat 7.7g, of which saturates 1.2g, of which polyunsaturates 4.3g; Cholesterol 281mg; Calcium 26mg; Fibre 0.3g; Sodium 1207mg.

MEAT AND POULTRY

Traditional South~east Asian curries tend to contain

relatively small amounts of meat and poultry, instead

being mainly based on vegetables, and served with

rice and noodles, making them an excellent low~fat

choice. Try the smooth Pork and Pineapple Curry or

the rich and flavoursome Duck in Spicy Orange

Sauce for a quick and tasty supper.

SWEET-AND-SOUR PORK STIR-FRY ★

THIS IS A GREAT IDEA FOR A QUICK FAMILY SUPPER. REMEMBER TO CUT THE CARROTS INTO THIN
MATCHSTICK STRIPS SO THAT THEY COOK IN TIME WITH THE REST OF THE INGREDIENTS.

SERVES FOUR

INGREDIENTS
    450g/1lb lean pork fillet (tenderloin)
    30ml/2 tbsp plain (all-purpose) flour
    5ml/1 tsp sunflower oil
    1 onion, roughly chopped
    1 garlic clove, crushed
    1 green (bell) pepper, seeded
      and sliced
    350g/12oz carrots, cut into
      thin strips
    225g/8oz can bamboo shoots, drained
    15ml/1 tbsp white wine vinegar
    15ml/1 tbsp soft brown sugar
    10ml/2 tsp tomato purée (paste)
    30ml/2 tbsp light soy sauce
    salt and ground black pepper

1 Thinly slice the pork. Season the flour and toss the pork in it to coat.

2 Heat the oil and cook the pork for 5 minutes, until golden. Remove the pork and drain on kitchen paper. You may need to do this in several batches.

3 Add the onion and garlic to the pan and cook for 3 minutes. Stir in the pepper and carrots and stir-fry over a high heat for 6–8 minutes, or until beginning to soften slightly.

4 Return the meat to the pan with the bamboo shoots. Add the remaining ingredients with 120ml/4fl oz/½ cup water and bring to the boil. Simmer gently for 2–3 minutes, or until piping hot. Adjust the seasoning, if necessary, and serve immediately.

VARIATION
Finely sliced strips of skinless chicken breast fillet can be used in this recipe instead of the pork.

Energy 235kcal/988kJ; Protein 25.3g; Carbohydrate 23.9g, of which sugars 16.2g; Fat 4.9g, of which saturates 1.6g, of which polyunsaturates 1.1g; Cholesterol 63mg; Calcium 62mg; Fibre 4.2g; Sodium 637mg.

STIR-FRIED PORK WITH DRIED SHRIMP ★★

YOU MIGHT EXPECT THE DRIED SHRIMP TO GIVE THIS DISH A FISHY FLAVOUR, BUT INSTEAD IT SIMPLY IMPARTS A DELICIOUS SAVOURY TASTE TO THE MEAT. SERVE WITH FRAGRANT STEAMED RICE.

SERVES FOUR

INGREDIENTS

  250g/9oz lean pork fillet
  (tenderloin), sliced
  15ml/1 tbsp sunflower oil
  2 garlic cloves, finely chopped
  45ml/3 tbsp dried shrimp
  10ml/2 tsp dried shrimp paste or
  5mm/¼ in piece from block of
  shrimp paste
  30ml/2 tbsp soy sauce
  juice of 1 lime
  15ml/1 tbsp palm sugar or light
  muscovado (brown) sugar
  1 small fresh red or green chilli,
  seeded and finely chopped
  4 pak choi (bok choy) or 450g/1lb
  spring greens (collards), shredded

1 Place the pork in the freezer for about 30 minutes, until firm. Using a sharp knife, cut it into thin slices.

2 Heat the oil in a wok or frying pan and cook the garlic until golden brown. Add the pork and stir-fry for about 4 minutes, until just cooked through.

3 Add the dried shrimp, then stir in the shrimp paste, with the soy sauce, lime juice and sugar. Add the chilli and pak choi or spring greens and toss over the heat until the vegetables are just wilted.

4 Transfer the stir-fry to warm individual bowls and serve immediately.

Energy 175kcal/731kJ; Protein 23.1g; Carbohydrate 6.3g, of which sugars 6.2g; Fat 6.4g, of which saturates 1.4g, of which polyunsaturates 2.8g; Cholesterol 96mg; Calcium 334mg; Fibre 2.4g; Sodium 1223mg.

SAENG WA OF GRILLED PORK ★

PORK FILLET IS CUT IN STRIPS BEFORE BEING GRILLED. SHREDDED AND THEN TOSSED WITH A DELICIOUS SWEET-SOUR SAUCE, IT MAKES A MARVELLOUS WARM SALAD.

SERVES FOUR

INGREDIENTS

  30ml/2 tbsp dark soy sauce
  15ml/1 tbsp clear honey
  400g/14oz pork fillet (tenderloin)
  6 shallots, very thinly
    sliced lengthways
  1 lemon grass stalk, thinly sliced
  5 kaffir lime leaves, thinly sliced
  5cm/2in piece fresh root ginger,
    peeled and sliced into
    fine shreds
  ½ fresh long red chilli, seeded and
    sliced into fine shreds
  small bunch fresh coriander
    (cilantro), chopped
For the dressing
  30ml/2 tbsp palm sugar or light
    muscovado (brown) sugar
  30ml/2 tbsp Thai fish sauce
  juice of 2 limes
  20ml/4 tsp thick tamarind juice,
    made by mixing tamarind paste
    with warm water

1 Preheat the grill (broiler) to medium. Mix the soy sauce with the honey in a small bowl or jug (pitcher) and stir until the honey has completely dissolved.

2 Using a sharp knife, cut the pork fillet lengthways into quarters to make four long, thick strips. Place the pork strips in a grill pan. Brush generously with the soy sauce and honey mixture, then grill (broil) for about 10–15 minutes, until cooked through and tender. Turn the strips over frequently and baste with the soy sauce and honey mixture.

3 Transfer the cooked pork strips to a board. Slice the meat across the grain, then shred it with a fork. Place in a large bowl and add the shallot slices, lemon grass, kaffir lime leaves, ginger, chilli and chopped coriander.

4 Make the dressing. Place the sugar, fish sauce, lime juice and tamarind juice in a bowl. Whisk until the sugar has completely dissolved. Pour the dressing over the pork mixture and toss well to mix, then serve.

VARIATION

If you want to extend this dish a little, add cooked rice or noodles. Thin strips of red or yellow (bell) pepper could also be added. For a colour contrast, add lightly cooked green beans, sugar snap peas or mangetouts (snow peas).

Energy 182kcal/767kJ; Protein 22.6g; Carbohydrate 14.3g, of which sugars 13.5g; Fat 4.2g, of which saturates 1.4g, of which polyunsaturates 0.7g; Cholesterol 63mg; Calcium 45mg; Fibre 1g; Sodium 1144mg.

STIR-FRIED PORK AND BUTTERNUT CURRY ★

THIS CURRY CAN BE MADE WITH BUTTERNUT SQUASH, PUMPKIN OR WINTER MELON. FLAVOURED WITH GALANGAL AND TURMERIC, IT IS DELICIOUS SERVED WITH RICE AND A FRUIT-BASED SALAD.

SERVES SIX

INGREDIENTS

10ml/2 tsp sunflower oil
25g/1oz galangal, finely sliced
2 red Thai chillies, peeled, seeded and finely sliced
3 shallots, halved and finely sliced
30ml/2 tbsp *kroeung*
10ml/2 tsp ground turmeric
5ml/1 tsp ground fenugreek
10ml/2 tsp palm sugar
450g/1lb lean pork loin, cut into bitesize chunks
30ml/2 tbsp *tuk prahoc*
900ml/1½ pints/3¾ cups reduced-fat coconut milk
1 butternut squash, peeled, seeded and cut into bitesize chunks
4 kaffir lime leaves
sea salt and ground black pepper
1 small bunch fresh coriander (cilantro), coarsely chopped and 1 small bunch fresh mint, stalks removed, to garnish
rice or noodles and salad, to serve

1 Heat the oil in a large wok or heavy pan. Stir in the galangal, chillies and shallots and stir-fry until fragrant. Add the *kroeung* and stir-fry until it begins to colour. Add the turmeric, fenugreek and sugar.

VARIATION

For a vegetarian option, omit the pork and use baby aubergines (eggplants) instead. The Cambodian flavourings and creamy coconut milk work well with many combinations.

2 Stir in the chunks of pork loin and stir-fry until golden brown on all sides. Stir in the *tuk prahoc* and pour in the coconut milk.

COOK'S TIP

Increase the number of chillies if you want a really hot curry.

3 Bring to the boil, add the squash and the lime leaves, and reduce the heat. Cook gently, uncovered, for 15–20 minutes, until the squash and pork are tender and the sauce has reduced. Season to taste. Garnish the curry with the coriander and mint, and serve with rice or noodles and salad.

Energy 149kcal/628kJ; Protein 17g; Carbohydrate 10.6g, of which sugars 10.2g; Fat 4.6g, of which saturates 1.5g, of which polyunsaturates 1.2g; Cholesterol 47mg; Calcium 71mg; Fibre 0.7g; Sodium 221mg.

PORK AND PINEAPPLE COCONUT CURRY ★

THE HEAT OF THIS CURRY BALANCES OUT ITS SWEETNESS TO MAKE A SMOOTH AND FRAGRANT DISH.
IT TAKES VERY LITTLE TIME TO COOK, SO IS IDEAL FOR A QUICK MID-WEEK SUPPER.

SERVES FOUR

INGREDIENTS

- 400ml/14fl oz reduced-fat coconut milk
- 10ml/2 tsp Thai red curry paste
- 400g/14oz lean pork loin steaks, trimmed and thinly sliced
- 15ml/1 tbsp Thai fish sauce
- 5ml/1 tsp palm sugar or light muscovado (brown) sugar
- 15ml/1 tbsp tamarind juice, made by mixing tamarind paste with warm water
- 2 kaffir lime leaves, torn
- ½ medium pineapple, peeled and chopped
- 1 fresh red chilli, seeded and finely chopped

1 Pour the coconut milk into a bowl and let it settle, so that the cream rises to the surface. Scoop the cream into a measuring jug (cup). You should have about 250ml/8fl oz/1 cup. If necessary, add a little of the coconut milk.

2 Pour the coconut cream into a large pan and bring it to the boil.

3 Cook the coconut cream for about 10 minutes, until the cream separates, stirring frequently to prevent it from sticking to the base of the pan and scorching. Add the red curry paste and stir until well mixed. Cook, stirring occasionally, for about 4 minutes, until the paste is fragrant.

4 Add the sliced pork and stir in the fish sauce, sugar and tamarind juice. Cook, stirring constantly, for 1–2 minutes, until the sugar has dissolved and the pork is no longer pink.

5 Add the remaining coconut milk and the lime leaves. Bring to the boil, then stir in the pineapple. Reduce the heat and simmer gently for 3 minutes, or until the pork is fully cooked. Sprinkle over the chilli and serve.

Energy 189kcal/800kJ; Protein 22.1g; Carbohydrate 16.1g, of which sugars 16.1g; Fat 4.5g, of which saturates 1.6g, of which polyunsaturates 0.8g; Cholesterol 63mg; Calcium 55mg; Fibre 1.2g; Sodium 182mg.

FRIED RICE <u>WITH</u> BEEF ★★

ONE OF THE JOYS OF THAI COOKING IS THE EASE AND SPEED WITH WHICH A REALLY GOOD MEAL CAN BE PREPARED. USING LEFT OVER COOKED RICE, THIS DISH CAN BE ON THE TABLE IN 15 MINUTES.

SERVES FOUR

INGREDIENTS
  200g/7oz lean beef steak
  5ml/1 tsp sunflower oil
  2 garlic cloves, finely chopped
  1 egg
  250g/9oz/2¼ cups cooked
    jasmine rice
  ½ medium head broccoli,
    coarsely chopped
  30ml/2 tbsp dark soy sauce
  15ml/1 tbsp light soy sauce
  5ml/1 tsp palm sugar or light
    muscovado (brown) sugar
  15ml/1 tbsp Thai fish sauce
  ground black pepper
  chilli sauce, to serve

1 Trim the steak and cut into very thin strips with a sharp knife.

2 Heat the oil in a wok or frying pan and cook the garlic over a low to medium heat until golden. Do not let it burn. Increase the heat to high, add the steak and stir-fry for 2 minutes.

3 Move the pieces of beef to the edges of the wok or pan and break the egg into the centre. When the egg starts to set, stir-fry it with the meat.

4 Add the rice and toss all the contents of the wok together, scraping up any residue on the base, then add the broccoli, soy sauces, sugar and fish sauce and stir-fry for 2 minutes more. Season to taste with pepper and serve immediately with chilli sauce.

COOK'S TIP
Soy sauce is made from fermented soya beans. The first extraction is sold as light soy sauce and has a delicate, "beany" fragrance. Dark soy sauce has been allowed to mature for longer.

Energy 232kcal/975kJ; Protein 16.9g; Carbohydrate 24.5g, of which sugars 5g; Fat 8.1g, of which saturates 2.7g, of which polyunsaturates 1.4g; Cholesterol 77mg; Calcium 52mg; Fibre 1.4g; Sodium 321mg.

CHILLI AND HONEY-CURED DRIED BEEF ★★

DRYING IS AN ANCIENT METHOD OF PRESERVING FOOD, WHICH ALSO INTENSIFIES THE FLAVOUR OR POTENCY OF MOST INGREDIENTS. IN THIS TRADITIONAL DISH THE CHILLIES ADD A WONDERFUL KICK TO THE MEAT WHILE THE HONEY ADDS A SUBTLE SWEETNESS.

2 Using a mortar and pestle, grind the chopped lemon grass, garlic and chillies to a paste. Stir in the honey, *nuoc mam* and soy sauce. Put the beef into a bowl, add the paste and rub it into the meat. Spread out the meat on a wire rack and place it in the refrigerator, uncovered, for 2 days, or until dry and hard.

3 Cook the dried beef on the barbecue or under a conventional grill (broiler) until heated through, and serve it with rice wrappers, fresh herbs and a dipping sauce.

COOK'S TIP
Drying is an ancient method of preserving food, which also intensifies the flavour or potency of most ingredients. In hot countries beef can be dried quickly in the sun, but in cooler areas it dries more slowly, so needs to be put in the refrigerator to prevent it going off.

VARIATION
This recipe also works well with venison. Cut the meat into thin strips and you have a South-east Asian version of the South African *biltong*.

SERVES SIX

INGREDIENTS
    450g/1lb lean beef sirloin
    2 lemon grass stalks, trimmed
      and chopped
    2 garlic cloves, chopped
    2 dried Serrano chillies, seeded
      and chopped
    30–45ml/2–3 tbsp honey
    15ml/1 tbsp *nuoc mam*
    30ml/2 tbsp soy sauce
    rice wrappers, fresh herbs and
      dipping sauce, to serve

1 Trim the beef and cut it across the grain into thin, rectangular slices, then set it aside.

Energy 158kcal/660kJ; Protein 17.3g; Carbohydrate 6.7g, of which sugars 6.6g; Fat 7g, of which saturates 2.9g, of which polyunsaturates 0.3g; Cholesterol 44mg; Calcium 6mg; Fibre 0.1g; Sodium 405mg.

SEARED BEEF SALAD IN A LIME DRESSING ★★

THIS BEEF DISH IS AN INDO-CHINESE FAVOURITE AND VERSIONS OF IT ARE ENJOYED IN VIETNAM, THAILAND, CAMBODIA AND LAOS. IT IS ALSO ONE OF THE TRADITIONAL DISHES THAT APPEAR IN THE BEEF SEVEN WAYS FEAST IN WHICH SEVEN DIFFERENT BEEF DISHES ARE SERVED.

SERVES SIX

INGREDIENTS
  about 7.5ml/1½ tsp sunflower oil
  450g/1lb beef fillet, cut into steaks
    2.5cm/1in thick
  115g/4oz/½ cup beansprouts
  1 bunch each fresh basil and mint,
    stalks removed, leaves shredded
  1 lime, cut into slices, to serve
For the dressing
  grated rind and juice (about
    80ml/3fl oz) of 2 limes
  30ml/2 tbsp *nuoc mam*
  30ml/2 tbsp raw cane sugar
  2 garlic cloves, crushed
  2 lemon grass stalks, finely sliced
  2 red Serrano chillies, seeded and
    finely sliced

3 Drain the meat of any excess juice and transfer it to a wide serving bowl. Add the beansprouts and herbs and toss it all together. Serve with lime slices to squeeze over.

1 To make the dressing, beat the lime rind, juice and *nuoc mam* in a bowl with the sugar, until the sugar dissolves. Stir in the garlic, lemon grass and chillies and set aside.

2 Pour a little oil into a heavy pan and rub it over the base with a piece of kitchen paper. Heat the pan and sear the steaks for 1–2 minutes each side. Transfer them to a board and leave to cool a little. Using a sharp knife, cut the meat into thin slices. Toss the slices in the dressing, cover and leave to marinate for 1–2 hours.

COOK'S TIP
It is worth buying an excellent-quality piece of tender beef fillet for this recipe as the meat is just seared.

Energy 174kcal/727kJ; Protein 18.4g; Carbohydrate 7.3g, of which sugars 6g; Fat 8.1g, of which saturates 3g, of which polyunsaturates 0.9g; Cholesterol 44mg; Calcium 28mg; Fibre 1g; Sodium 52mg.

GREEN CHICKEN CURRY ★★

USE ONE OR TWO FRESH GREEN CHILLIES IN THIS DISH, DEPENDING ON HOW HOT YOU LIKE YOUR CURRY. THE MILD AROMATIC FLAVOUR OF THE RICE IS A GOOD FOIL FOR THE SPICY CHICKEN.

SERVES FOUR

INGREDIENTS
- 4 spring onions (scallions), trimmed and coarsely chopped
- 1–2 fresh green chillies, seeded and coarsely chopped
- 2cm/¾ in piece fresh root ginger, peeled
- 2 garlic cloves
- 5ml/1 tsp Thai fish sauce
- large bunch fresh coriander (cilantro)
- small handful of fresh parsley or 1 lemon grass stalk, chopped into 4 sticks and lightly crushed
- 30–45ml/2–3 tbsp water
- 15ml/1 tbsp sunflower oil
- 4 skinless, chicken breast fillets, diced
- 1 green (bell) pepper, seeded and thinly sliced
- 600ml/1 pint/2½ cups reduced-fat coconut milk
- salt and ground black pepper
- hot coconut rice, to serve

1 Put the spring onions, chillies, ginger, garlic, fish sauce, coriander and parsley or lemon grass in a food processor or blender. Pour in 30ml/2 tbsp of the water and process to a smooth paste, adding a further 15ml/1 tbsp water if required.

COOK'S TIP
Virtually every Thai cook has their own recipe for curry pastes, which are traditionally made by pounding the ingredients in a mortar with a pestle. Using a food processor or blender simply makes the task less laborious.

2 Heat half the oil in a large frying pan. Cook the diced chicken until evenly browned. Transfer to a plate.

3 Heat the remaining oil in the frying pan. Add the thinly sliced green pepper and stir-fry for 3–4 minutes, then add the chilli and ginger paste. Stir-fry for 3–4 minutes, until the mixture becomes fairly thick.

4 Return the chicken to the pan and add the reduced-fat coconut milk. Season with salt and pepper to taste and bring to the boil, then reduce the heat, half cover the pan and simmer for 8–10 minutes.

5 When the chicken is cooked, transfer it, with the green pepper, to a plate. Boil the cooking liquid remaining in the pan for 10–12 minutes, until it is well reduced and fairly thick.

6 Return the chicken and green pepper to the green curry sauce, stir well and cook gently for 2–3 minutes to heat through thoroughly. Spoon the curry over the coconut rice, and serve immediately.

Energy 208kcal/877kJ; Protein 28g; Carbohydrate 8g, of which sugars 7.9g; Fat 7.4g, of which saturates 1.3g, of which polyunsaturates 3.7g; Cholesterol 79mg; Calcium 76mg; Fibre 0.7g; Sodium 237mg.

CHICKEN AND BASIL COCONUT RICE ★

FOR THIS DISH, THE THAI FRAGRANT RICE IS PARTIALLY BOILED BEFORE BEING SIMMERED WITH COCONUT SO THAT IT FULLY ABSORBS THE FLAVOUR OF THE CHILLIES, BASIL AND SPICES.

SERVES FOUR

INGREDIENTS
   350g/12oz/1¾ cups Thai fragrant
      rice, rinsed
   15ml/1 tbsp sunflower oil
   1 large onion, finely sliced into rings
   1 garlic clove, crushed
   1 fresh red chilli, seeded and
      finely sliced
   1 fresh green chilli, seeded and
      finely sliced
   generous handful of basil leaves
   3 skinless chicken breast fillets,
      about 350g/12oz, finely sliced
   5mm/¼in piece of lemon grass,
      pounded or finely chopped
   600ml/1 pint/2½ cups reduced-fat
      coconut milk
   salt and ground black pepper

1 Bring a pan of lightly salted water to the boil. Add the rice to the pan and boil for about 6 minutes, until partially cooked. Drain and set aside.

2 Heat the oil in a frying pan and fry the onion rings for 5–10 minutes until golden and crisp. Lift out, drain on kitchen paper and set aside.

3 Fry the garlic and chillies in the oil remaining in the pan for 2–3 minutes, then add the basil leaves and fry briefly until they begin to wilt.

4 Remove a few basil leaves and set them aside for the garnish, then add the chicken slices with the lemon grass and fry for 2–3 minutes until golden. Add the rice. Stir-fry for a few minutes to coat the grains, then pour in the coconut cream. Cook for 4–5 minutes or until the rice is tender, adding a little more water if necessary. Adjust the seasoning.

5 Pile the rice into a warmed serving dish or in a halved coconut if you like, sprinkle with the fried onion rings and basil leaves, and serve immediately.

Energy 492kcal/2064kJ; Protein 28.8g; Carbohydrate 83.1g, of which sugars 11.6g; Fat 4.8g, of which saturates 0.9g, of which polyunsaturates 2g; Cholesterol 61mg; Calcium 83mg; Fibre 1.1g; Sodium 220mg.

STIR-FRIED CHICKEN WITH BASIL AND CHILLI ★

THAI BASIL, WHICH IS SOMETIMES KNOWN AS HOLY BASIL, HAS A UNIQUE, PUNGENT FLAVOUR THAT IS BOTH SPICY AND SHARP. SKINLESS, BONELESS CHICKEN BREAST FILLETS ARE ESPECIALLY LOW IN FAT.

2 Add the pieces of chicken to the wok or pan, in batches if necessary, and stir-fry until the chicken changes colour.

3 Stir in the fish sauce, soy sauce and sugar. Continue to stir-fry the mixture for 3–4 minutes, or until the chicken is fully cooked and golden brown.

4 Stir in the fresh Thai basil leaves. Spoon the mixture on to a warm platter, or into individual dishes. Garnish with the chopped chillies and deep-fried Thai basil and serve immediately.

SERVES SIX

INGREDIENTS

- 15ml/1 tbsp sunflower oil
- 4 garlic cloves, thinly sliced
- 2–4 fresh red chillies, seeded and finely chopped
- 450g/1lb skinless chicken breast fillets, cut into bitesize pieces
- 45ml/3 tbsp Thai fish sauce
- 10ml/2 tsp dark soy sauce
- 5ml/1 tsp granulated sugar
- 10–12 fresh Thai basil leaves
- 2 fresh red chillies, seeded and finely chopped, and 18 deep-fried Thai basil leaves, to garnish (optional)

1 Heat the oil in a wok or large, heavy frying pan. Add the garlic and chillies and stir-fry over a medium heat for 1–2 minutes until the garlic is golden. Take care not to let the garlic burn, otherwise it will taste bitter.

COOK'S TIP

To deep-fry Thai basil leaves, first make sure that the leaves are completely dry or they will splutter when they are added to the oil. Heat vegetable or sunflower oil in a wok or deep-fryer to 190°C/375°F or until a cube of bread, added to the oil, browns in about 45 seconds. Add the leaves and deep-fry them briefly until they are crisp and translucent – this will take only about 30–40 seconds. Lift out the leaves using a slotted spoon or wire basket. Drain them well on kitchen paper before using.

Energy 113kcal/474kJ; Protein 19.1g; Carbohydrate 2.9g, of which sugars 1.6g; Fat 2.8g, of which saturates 0.5g, of which polyunsaturates 1.3g; Cholesterol 53mg; Calcium 22mg; Fibre 0.7g; Sodium 582mg.

CHICKEN AND LEMON GRASS CURRY ★

THIS AROMATIC AND TRULY DELICIOUS CURRY IS EXCEPTIONALLY EASY AND VERY QUICK TO MAKE.
IT TAKES LESS THAN TWENTY MINUTES TO PREPARE AND COOK — A PERFECT MID-WEEK MEAL.

SERVES FOUR

INGREDIENTS

10ml/2 tsp sunflower oil
2 garlic cloves, crushed
500g/1¼lb skinless, boneless
    chicken thighs, chopped into
    small pieces
45ml/3 tbsp Thai fish sauce
120ml/4fl oz/½ cup
    chicken stock
5ml/1 tsp granulated sugar
1 lemon grass stalk, chopped into
    4 sticks and lightly crushed
5 kaffir lime leaves, rolled into
    cylinders and thinly sliced across,
    plus extra to garnish
chopped roasted peanuts
    and chopped fresh coriander
    (cilantro), to garnish

For the curry paste
1 lemon grass stalk,
    coarsely chopped
2.5cm/1in piece fresh galangal,
    peeled and coarsely chopped
2 kaffir lime leaves, chopped
3 shallots, coarsely chopped
6 coriander (cilantro) roots,
    coarsely chopped
2 garlic cloves
2 fresh green chillies, seeded and
    coarsely chopped
5ml/1 tsp shrimp paste
5ml/1 tsp ground turmeric

1 Make the curry paste. Place all the ingredients in a large mortar, or food processor and pound with a pestle or process to a smooth paste.

2 Heat the sunflower oil in a wok or large, heavy frying pan, add the garlic and cook over a low heat, stirring frequently, until golden brown. Be careful not to let the garlic burn or it will taste bitter. Add the curry paste and stir-fry with the garlic for about 30 seconds more.

3 Add the chicken pieces to the pan and stir until thoroughly coated with the curry paste. Stir in the Thai fish sauce and chicken stock, with the sugar, and cook, stirring constantly, for 2 minutes more.

4 Add the lemon grass and lime leaves, reduce the heat and simmer for 10 minutes. If the mixture begins to dry out, add a little more stock or water.

5 Remove the lemon grass, if you like. Spoon the curry into four dishes, garnish with the lime leaves, peanuts and coriander and serve immediately.

Energy 122kcal/512kJ; Protein 17.4g; Carbohydrate 3.7g, of which sugars 3g; Fat 4.3g, of which saturates 0.8g, of which polyunsaturates 1.6g; Cholesterol 85mg; Calcium 77mg; Fibre 1.6g; Sodium 131mg.

RED CHICKEN CURRY WITH BAMBOO SHOOTS ★

BAMBOO SHOOTS HAVE A LOVELY CRUNCHY TEXTURE. IT IS QUITE ACCEPTABLE TO USE CANNED ONES, AS FRESH BAMBOO IS NOT READILY AVAILABLE IN THE WEST. BUY CANNED WHOLE BAMBOO SHOOTS, WHICH ARE CRISPER AND OF BETTER QUALITY THAN SLICED SHOOTS. RINSE BEFORE USING.

SERVES SIX

INGREDIENTS
475ml/16fl oz/2 cups reduced-fat coconut milk
450g/1lb skinless chicken fillets, cut into bitesize pieces
30ml/2 tbsp Thai fish sauce
15ml/1 tbsp sugar
475ml/16fl oz/2 cups chicken stock
225g/8oz drained canned bamboo shoots, rinsed and sliced
5 kaffir lime leaves, torn
chopped fresh red chillies and kaffir lime leaves, to garnish
For the red curry paste
5ml/1 tsp coriander seeds
2.5ml/½ tsp cumin seeds
12–15 fresh red chillies, seeded and roughly chopped
4 shallots, thinly sliced
2 garlic cloves, chopped
15ml/1 tbsp chopped galangal
2 lemon grass stalks, chopped
3 kaffir lime leaves, chopped
4 fresh coriander (cilantro) roots
10 black peppercorns
good pinch of ground cinnamon
5ml/1 tsp ground turmeric
2.5ml/½ tsp shrimp paste
5ml/1 tsp salt
15ml/1 tbsp sunflower oil

2 Add the oil, a little at a time, mixing or processing well after each addition. Transfer to a jar and keep in the refrigerator until ready to use.

3 Pour the coconut milk into a large heavy pan. Bring the milk to the boil, stirring constantly until it has separated.

1 Make the red curry paste. Dry-fry the coriander and cumin seeds for 1–2 minutes, then put in a mortar with the remaining ingredients except the oil and pound to a paste.

4 Stir in 30ml/2 tbsp of the red curry paste and cook the mixture for 2–3 minutes, stirring constantly. Remaining red curry paste can be kept in the refrigerator for up to 3 months.

5 Add the chicken fillets, Thai fish sauce and sugar to the pan. Stir well, then cook for 5–6 minutes until the chicken changes colour and is lightly golden and cooked through. Stir the chicken constantly to prevent the mixture from sticking to the bottom of the pan.

6 Pour the chicken stock into the pan, then add the sliced bamboo shoots and the torn kaffir lime leaves. Bring back to the boil over a medium heat, stirring constantly to prevent the chicken from sticking. Then remove the curry from the heat and season with salt and pepper to taste if necessary.

7 To serve, spoon the curry immediately into a warmed serving dish and garnish with chopped red chillies and kaffir lime leaves.

VARIATION
Instead of, or as well as, bamboo shoots, use straw mushrooms. These are available as dried mushrooms or in cans from Asian stores and supermarkets. Whether you are using dried or canned mushrooms, stir into the dish a few minutes before serving the curry.

COOK'S TIP
It is essential to use chicken breast fillets, rather than any other cut, for this curry, as it is cooked very quickly. Look out for diced chicken or strips of chicken (which are often labelled "stir-fry chicken") in the supermarket.

Energy 131kcal/552kJ; Protein 18.8g; Carbohydrate 7.5g, of which sugars 7.2g; Fat 3g, of which saturates 0.6g, of which polyunsaturates 1.3g; Cholesterol 55mg; Calcium 51mg; Fibre 0.5g; Sodium 153mg.

SPICY CHICKEN WITH YOUNG GINGER ★★

GINGER PLAYS A BIG ROLE IN CAMBODIAN COOKING, PARTICULARLY IN THE STIR-FRIED DISHES. WHENEVER POSSIBLE, THE JUICIER AND MORE PUNGENT YOUNG GINGER IS USED.

SERVES FOUR

INGREDIENTS

15ml/1 tbsp sunflower oil
3 garlic cloves, finely sliced
  in strips
50g/2oz fresh young root ginger,
  finely sliced in strips
2 Thai chillies, seeded and finely
  sliced in strips
4 skinless chicken fillets or 4 boned
  chicken legs, skinned and cut
  into bitesize chunks
30ml/2 tbsp *tuk prahoc*
10ml/2 tsp sugar
1 small bunch coriander (cilantro),
  stalks removed, roughly chopped
ground black pepper
jasmine rice and crunchy salad or
  baguette, to serve

1 Heat a wok or heavy pan and add the oil. Add the garlic, ginger and chillies, and stir-fry until fragrant and golden. Add the chicken and toss it around the wok for 1–2 minutes.

COOK'S TIP
Young ginger is available in Chinese and South-east Asian markets.

2 Stir in the *tuk prahoc* and sugar, and stir-fry for a further 4–5 minutes until cooked. Season with pepper and add some of the fresh coriander. Transfer the chicken to a serving dish and garnish with the remaining coriander. Serve hot with jasmine rice and a crunchy salad with fresh herbs, or with chunks of freshly baked baguette.

Energy 187kcal/786kJ; Protein 27.5g; Carbohydrate 1g, of which sugars 3.8g, Fat 6.9g, of which saturates 1g, of which polyunsaturates 3.7g; Cholesterol 79mg; Calcium 35mg; Fibre 0.9g; Sodium 75mg.

JUNGLE CURRY OF GUINEA FOWL ★

A TRADITIONAL WILD FOOD COUNTRY CURRY FROM THE NORTH-CENTRAL REGION OF THAILAND, THIS DISH CAN BE MADE USING ANY GAME, FISH OR CHICKEN.

SERVES FOUR

INGREDIENTS

- 1 guinea fowl or similar game bird
- 10ml/2 tsp sunflower oil
- 10ml/2 tsp green curry paste
- 15ml/1 tbsp Thai fish sauce
- 2.5cm/1in piece fresh galangal, peeled and finely chopped
- 15ml/1 tbsp fresh green peppercorns
- 3 kaffir lime leaves, torn
- 15ml/1 tbsp whisky, preferably Mekhong
- 300ml/½ pint/1¼ cups chicken stock
- 50g/2oz snake beans or yard-long beans, cut into 2.5cm/1in lengths (about ½ cup)
- 225g/8oz/3¼ cups chestnut mushrooms, sliced
- 1 piece drained canned bamboo shoot, about 50g/2oz, shredded
- 5ml/1 tsp dried chilli flakes, to garnish (optional)

1 Cut up the guinea fowl, remove and discard the skin, then take all the meat off the bones. Chop the meat into bitesize pieces and set aside.

2 Heat the oil in a wok or frying pan and add the curry paste. Stir-fry over a medium heat for 30 seconds.

3 Add the fish sauce and the guinea fowl meat and stir-fry until the meat is browned all over. Add the galangal, peppercorns, lime leaves and whisky, then pour in the stock.

4 Bring to the boil. Add the vegetables, return to a simmer and cook gently for 2–3 minutes, until they are just cooked. Spoon into a dish, sprinkle with chilli flakes, if you like, and serve.

COOK'S TIPS

- Guinea fowl range from 675g/1½ lb to 2kg/4½ lb, but 1.2kg/2½ lb is average. American readers could substitute two or three Cornish hens, depending on size.
- Bottled green peppercorns can be used as a substitute for fresh green peppercorns, but rinse well and drain them first.

Energy 200kcal/846kJ; Protein 38.5g; Carbohydrate 7.1g, of which sugars 4.9g; Fat 2.2g, of which saturates 0.5g, of which polyunsaturates 0.6g; Cholesterol 105mg; Calcium 37mg; Fibre 2.1g; Sodium 96mg.

MARINATED DUCK CURRY ★★

A richly spiced curry that illustrates the powerful Chinese influence on Thai cuisine. The duck is best marinated for as long as possible, although the flavour will be improved even if you only have time to marinate it briefly.

2 Meanwhile, bring a pan of water to the boil. Add the squash and cook for 10–15 minutes, until just tender. Drain well and set aside.

3 Pour the marinade from the duck into a wok and heat until boiling. Stir in the curry paste and cook for 2–3 minutes, until well blended and fragrant. Add the duck and cook for 3–4 minutes, stirring constantly, until browned on all sides.

4 Add the fish sauce and palm sugar and cook for 2 minutes more. Stir in the coconut milk until the mixture is smooth, then add the cooked squash, with the chillies and lime leaves.

5 Simmer gently, stirring frequently, for 5 minutes, then spoon into a dish, sprinkle with the coriander and serve.

VARIATION
This dish works just as well with skinless chicken breast fillets.

SERVES FOUR

INGREDIENTS
   4 duck breast portions, skin and
     bones removed
   30ml/2 tbsp five-spice powder
   15ml/1 tbsp sesame oil
   grated rind and juice of 1 orange
   1 medium butternut squash, peeled
     and cubed
   10ml/2 tsp Thai red curry paste
   30ml/2 tbsp Thai fish sauce
   15ml/1 tbsp palm sugar
   300ml/½ pint/1¼ cups reduced-fat
     coconut milk
   2 fresh red chillies, seeded
   4 kaffir lime leaves, torn
   small bunch coriander (cilantro),
     chopped, to garnish

1 Cut the duck meat into bitesize pieces and place in a bowl with the five-spice powder, sesame oil and orange rind and juice. Stir well to mix all the ingredients and coat the duck in the marinade. Cover the bowl with clear film (plastic wrap) and set aside in a cool place to marinate for at least 15 minutes.

Energy 182kcal/767kJ; Protein 20.3g; Carbohydrate 7.9g, of which sugars 7.9g; Fat 9.6g, of which saturates 1.9g, of which polyunsaturates 1.8g; Cholesterol 110mg; Calcium 61mg; Fibre 0.6g; Sodium 197mg.

DUCK <u>IN A</u> SPICY ORANGE SAUCE ★★

DELICIOUSLY RICH IN FLAVOUR, DUCK CAN BE QUITE FATTY, MAKING THIS MEAT DIFFICULT FOR THOSE FOLLOWING A LOW-FAT DIET. TO REDUCE THE FAT CONTENT OF THIS DISH SIMPLY REMOVE THE SKIN BEFORE SERVING. SERVE WITH STEAMED RICE AND BRIGHT VEGETABLES.

SERVES FOUR

INGREDIENTS
4 duck legs
4 garlic cloves, crushed
50g/2oz fresh root ginger, peeled and
  finely sliced
2 lemon grass stalks, trimmed,
  cut into 3 pieces and crushed
2 dried whole red Thai chillies
15ml/1 tbsp palm sugar
5ml/1 tsp five-spice powder
30ml/2 tbsp *nuoc cham* or *tuk trey*
900ml/1½ pints/3¾ cups fresh
  orange juice
sea salt and ground black pepper
1 lime, cut into quarters

3 Stir in the orange juice and place the duck legs back in the pan. Cover the pan and gently cook the duck for 1–2 hours, until the meat is tender and the sauce has reduced. Season and serve with lime wedges to squeeze over it.

1 Place the duck legs, skin side down, in a large heavy pan or flameproof clay pot. Cook them on both sides over a medium heat for about 10 minutes, until browned and crispy. Transfer them to a plate and set aside.

2 Stir the garlic, ginger, lemon grass and chillies into the fat left in the pan, and cook until golden. Add the sugar, five-spice powder and *nuoc cham* or *tuk trey*.

Energy 234kcal/986kJ; Protein 22.1g; Carbohydrate 26g, of which sugars 24.2g; Fat 6.9g, of which saturates 1.3g, of which polyunsaturates 0.6g; Cholesterol 110mg; Calcium 59mg; Fibre 1.2g; Sodium 137mg.

RICE AND NOODLES

Low in fat and high in carbohydrate, rice and noodles
form the bulk of most meals in Thailand and South-
east Asia. Universally low in saturated fat, many of
these recipes contain all the delicious flavours of
classic Thai cooking but with less than 1 gram of fat
per serving. Mouthwatering dishes include Curried
Rice Vermicelli, and traditional Mixed Meat Noodles.

COCONUT RICE ★

THIS RICH DISH IS OFTEN SERVED WITH A TANGY PAPAYA SALAD TO BALANCE THE SWEETNESS OF THE COCONUT MILK AND SUGAR. IT IS ONE OF THOSE COMFORTING TREATS THAT EVERYONE ENJOYS.

SERVES SIX

INGREDIENTS
  250ml/8fl oz/1 cup water
  475ml/16fl oz/2 cups reduced-fat coconut milk
  2.5ml/½ tsp salt
  30ml/2 tbsp granulated sugar
  450g/1lb/2⅔ cups jasmine rice

COOK'S TIP
For a special occasion serve in a halved papaya and garnish with thin shreds of fresh coconut. Use a vegetable peeler to pare the coconut finely.

1 Place the measured water, coconut milk, salt and sugar in a heavy pan. Wash the rice in several changes of cold water until it runs clear.

2 Add the jasmine rice, cover tightly with a lid and bring to the boil over a medium heat. Reduce the heat to low and simmer gently, without lifting the lid unnecessarily, for 15–20 minutes, until the rice is tender and cooked through. Test it by biting a grain.

3 Turn off the heat and leave the rice to rest in the pan, still covered with the lid, for a further 5–10 minutes.

4 Gently fluff up the rice grains with chopsticks or a fork before transferring it to a warmed dish and serving.

Energy 306kcal/1286kJ; Protein 5.8g; Carbohydrate 69g, of which sugars 9.1g; Fat 0.6g, of which saturates 0.2g, of which polyunsaturates 0g; Cholesterol 0mg; Calcium 40mg; Fibre 0g; Sodium 218mg.

JASMINE RICE WITH PRAWNS AND THAI BASIL ★★

THAI BASIL (BAI GRAPAO), ALSO KNOWN AS HOLY BASIL, HAS A UNIQUE, PUNGENT FLAVOUR THAT IS BOTH SPICY AND SHARP. IT CAN BE FOUND IN MOST ASIAN FOOD MARKETS.

SERVES SIX

INGREDIENTS

    15ml/1 tbsp sunflower oil
    1 egg, beaten
    1 onion, chopped
    15ml/1 tbsp chopped garlic
    15ml/1 tbsp shrimp paste
    1kg/2¼lb/4 cups cooked jasmine rice
    350g/12oz cooked shelled prawns
      (shrimp)
    50g/2oz thawed frozen peas
    oyster sauce, to taste
    2 spring onions (scallions), chopped
    15–20 Thai basil leaves, roughly
      snipped, plus an extra sprig,
      to garnish

1 Heat 15ml/1 tbsp of the oil in a wok or frying pan. Add the beaten egg and swirl it around to set like a thin omelette.

2 Cook the omelette (on one side only) over a gentle heat until golden. Slide the omelette on to a board, roll up and cut into thin strips. Set aside.

3 Heat the remaining oil in the wok or pan, add the onion and garlic and stir-fry for 2–3 minutes. Stir in the shrimp paste and mix well until thoroughly combined.

4 Add the rice, prawns and peas and toss and stir together, until everything is heated through.

5 Season with oyster sauce to taste, taking great care as the shrimp paste is salty. Mix in the spring onions and basil leaves. Transfer to a serving dish and top with the strips of omelette. Serve, garnished with a sprig of basil.

Energy 311kcal/1316kJ; Protein 16.3g; Carbohydrate 52.6g, of which sugars 0.3g; Fat 5.4g, of which saturates 1.1g, of which polyunsaturates 2.2g; Cholesterol 145mg; Calcium 84mg; Fibre 0.6g; Sodium 125mg.

FESTIVE RICE ★

THIS PRETTY THAI DISH IS TRADITIONALLY SHAPED INTO A CONE AND SURROUNDED BY A VARIETY OF ACCOMPANIMENTS BEFORE BEING SERVED. SERVE AT A HEALTHY SUMMERTIME LUNCH.

2 Heat the oil in a frying pan with a lid. Cook the garlic, onions and turmeric over a low heat for 2–3 minutes, until the onions have softened. Add the rice and stir well to coat in oil.

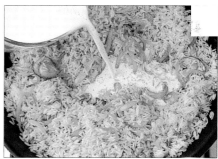

3 Pour in the water and coconut milk and add the lemon grass. Bring to the boil, stirring. Cover the pan and cook gently for 12 minutes, or until all the liquid has been absorbed by the rice.

4 Remove the pan from the heat and lift the lid. Cover with a clean dish towel, replace the lid and leave to stand in a warm place for 15 minutes. Remove the lemon grass, mound the rice mixture in a cone on a serving platter and garnish with the accompaniments, then serve.

SERVES EIGHT

INGREDIENTS
   450g/1lb/2⅔ cups jasmine rice
   30ml/2 tbsp sunflower oil
   2 garlic cloves, crushed
   2 onions, thinly sliced
   2.5ml/½ tsp ground turmeric
   750ml/1¼ pints/3 cups water
   400ml/14fl oz can reduced-fat
      coconut milk
   1–2 lemon grass stalks, bruised
For the accompaniments
   omelette strips
   2 fresh red chillies, shredded
   cucumber chunks
   tomato wedges
   fried onions
   prawn (shrimp) crackers

1 Put the jasmine rice in a large strainer and rinse it thoroughly under cold water. Drain well.

COOK'S TIP
Jasmine rice is widely available in most supermarkets and Asian stores. It is also known as Thai fragrant rice.

Energy 224kcal/939kJ; Protein 4.8g; Carbohydrate 49.5g, of which sugars 4g; Fat 0.6g, of which saturates 0.1g, of which polyunsaturates 0g; Cholesterol 0mg; Calcium 44mg; Fibre 0.7g; Sodium 58mg.

THAI FRIED RICE ★★

THIS SUBSTANTIAL AND TASTY DISH IS A GREAT ALTERNATIVE TO PLAIN RICE. DICED CHICKEN, RED
PEPPER, GINGER AND CORN KERNELS ADD COLOUR AND EXTRA FLAVOUR. CHILLI OIL ADDS SPICE.

SERVES FOUR

INGREDIENTS
   475ml/16fl oz/2 cups water
   50g/2oz/½ cup coconut
     milk powder
   350g/12oz/1¾ cups jasmine
     rice, rinsed
   15ml/1 tbsp sunflower oil
   2 garlic cloves, chopped
   1 small onion, finely chopped
   2.5cm/1in piece of fresh root ginger,
     peeled and grated
   225g/8oz skinless, chicken breast
     fillets, cut into 1cm/½in dice
   1 red (bell) pepper, seeded
     and sliced
   115g/4oz/1 cup drained canned
     whole kernel corn
   5ml/1 tsp chilli oil
   5ml/1 tsp hot curry powder
   2 eggs, beaten
   salt
   spring onion (scallion) shreds,
     to garnish

3 Push the onion mixture to the sides of the wok, add the chicken to the centre and stir-fry for 2 minutes. Add the rice and toss well. Stir-fry over a high heat for about 3 minutes more, until the chicken is cooked through.

4 Stir in the sliced red pepper, corn, chilli oil and curry powder, with salt to taste. Toss over the heat for 1 minute. Stir in the beaten eggs and cook for 1 minute more. Garnish with the spring onion shreds and serve.

1 Pour the water into a pan and whisk in the coconut milk powder. Add the rice and bring to the boil. Reduce the heat, cover and cook for 12 minutes, or until the rice is tender and the liquid has been absorbed. Spread the rice on a baking sheet and leave until cold.

2 Heat the oil in a wok, add the garlic, onion and ginger and stir-fry over a medium heat for 2 minutes.

COOK'S TIP
It is important that the rice is completely cold before being fried.

Energy 508kcal/2127kJ; Protein 24.7g; Carbohydrate 83.9g, of which sugars 8.7g; Fat 8g, of which saturates 1.6g, of which polyunsaturates 2.7g; Cholesterol 135mg; Calcium 57mg; Fibre 1.3g; Sodium 204mg.

GARLIC AND GINGER RICE WITH CORIANDER ★

In Vietnam and Cambodia, when rice is served on the side, it is usually steamed and plain, or fragrant with the flavours of ginger and herbs. The combination of garlic and ginger is popular in both countries and complements almost any vegetable, fish or meat dish.

SERVES SIX

INGREDIENTS
    15ml/1 tbsp sunflower oil
    2–3 garlic cloves,
        finely chopped
    25g/1oz fresh root ginger,
        finely chopped
    225g/8oz/generous 1 cup
        long grain rice, rinsed in
        several bowls of cold water
        and drained
    900ml/1½ pints/3¾ cups
        chicken stock
    a bunch of fresh coriander (cilantro)
        leaves, finely chopped
    a bunch of fresh basil and mint,
        (optional), finely chopped

1 Heat the oil in a clay pot or heavy pan. Stir in the garlic and ginger and fry until golden. Stir in the rice and allow it to absorb the flavours for 1–2 minutes. Pour in the stock and stir to make sure the rice doesn't stick. Bring the stock to the boil, then reduce the heat.

2 Sprinkle the coriander over the surface of the stock, cover the pan, and leave to cook gently for 20–25 minutes, until the rice has absorbed all the liquid. Turn off the heat and gently fluff up the rice to mix in the coriander. Cover and leave to infuse for 10 minutes before serving.

Energy 162kcal/677kJ; Protein 3.7g; Carbohydrate 31.5g, of which sugars 0.3g; Fat 2.2g, of which saturates 0.2g, of which polyunsaturates 1.2g; Cholesterol 0mg; Calcium 25mg; Fibre 0.8g; Sodium 3mg.

SPICED CHILLI RICE ★

ALTHOUGH PLAIN STEAMED RICE IS SERVED AT ALMOST EVERY MEAL THROUGHOUT SOUTHERN ASIA, MANY FAMILIES LIKE TO SNEAK IN A LITTLE SPICE TOO. A BURST OF CHILLI FOR FIRE, TURMERIC FOR COLOUR, AND CORIANDER FOR ITS COOLING FLAVOUR, ARE ALL THAT'S NEEDED.

SERVES FOUR

INGREDIENTS

  15ml/1 tbsp sunflower oil
  2–3 green or red Thai chillies,
    seeded and finely chopped
  2 garlic cloves, finely chopped
  2.5cm/1in fresh root ginger, chopped
  5ml/1 tsp sugar
  10–15ml/2–3 tsp ground turmeric
  225g/8oz/generous 1 cup long
    grain rice
  30ml/2 tbsp *nuoc mam*
  600ml/1 pint/2½ cups water
  1 bunch of fresh coriander
    (cilantro), stalks removed, leaves
    finely chopped
  salt and ground black pepper

1 Heat the oil in a heavy pan. Stir in the chillies, garlic and ginger with the sugar. As they begin to colour, stir in the turmeric. Add the rice, coating it well, then pour in the *nuoc mam* and the water – the liquid should sit about 2.5cm/1in above the rice.

2 Tip the rice on to a serving dish. Add some of the coriander and lightly toss together using a fork. Garnish with the remaining coriander.

COOK'S TIP
This rice goes well with grilled and stir-fried fish and shellfish dishes, but you can serve it as an alternative to plain rice. Add extra chillies, if you like.

3 Season with salt and ground black pepper and bring the liquid to the boil. Reduce the heat, cover and simmer for about 25 minutes, or until the water has been absorbed. Remove from the heat and leave the rice to steam for a further 10 minutes.

Energy 247kcal/1032kJ; Protein 5.5g; Carbohydrate 48.3g, of which sugars 1.5g; Fat 3.3g, of which saturates 0.4g, of which polyunsaturates 1.8g; Cholesterol 0mg; Calcium 39mg; Fibre 1.1g; Sodium 5mg.

RICE NOODLES WITH FRESH HERBS ★

THESE THIN, WIRY NOODLES ARE ALSO KNOWN AS AS RICE STICKS OR RICE VERMICELLI. THIS TASTY NOODLE SALAD CAN BE SERVED BY ITSELF OR AS AN ACCOMPANIMENT TO MEAT OR FISH DISHES.

SERVES FOUR

INGREDIENTS
 half a small cucumber
 225g/8oz dried rice sticks (vermicelli)
 4–6 lettuce leaves, shredded
 115g/4oz/½ cup beansprouts
 1 bunch mixed basil, coriander
  (cilantro), mint and oregano, stalks
  removed, leaves shredded
 juice of half a lime
 nuoc mam or *nuoc cham*, to drizzle

COOK'S TIP
In the street stalls and cafés of Hanoi, different types of mint, ginger leaves, oregano and thyme provide the herb bedding for this dish, giving it a really distinctive, fragrant flavour.

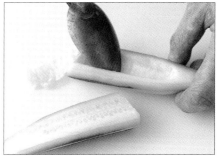

1 Peel the cucumber, cut it in half lengthways, remove the seeds, and cut into matchsticks.

2 Add the rice sticks to a pan of boiling water, loosening them gently, and cook for 3–4 minutes, or until *al dente*. Drain, rinse under cold water, and drain again.

3 In a bowl, toss the shredded lettuce, beansprouts, cucumber and herbs together. Add the noodles and lime juice and toss together. Drizzle with a little *nuoc mam* or *nuoc cham* for seasoning, and serve immediately on its own, or with stir-fried seafood or chicken as a complete meal.

Energy 225kcal/940kJ; Protein 6.9g; Carbohydrate 47.1g, of which sugars 2.5g; Fat 0.8g, of which saturates 0.1g, of which polyunsaturates 0.2g; Cholesterol 0mg; Calcium 66mg; Fibre 1.8g; Sodium 13mg.

SWEET AND HOT VEGETABLE NOODLES ★

THIS NOODLE DISH HAS THE COLOUR OF FIRE, BUT ONLY THE MILDEST SUGGESTION OF HEAT. GINGER AND PLUM SAUCE GIVE IT ITS FRUITY FLAVOUR, WHILE LIME ADDS A DELICIOUS TANG.

SERVES FOUR

INGREDIENTS

130g/4½oz dried rice noodles
15ml/1 tbsp sunflower oil
2.5cm/1in piece fresh root ginger,
   sliced into thin batons
1 garlic clove, crushed
130g/4½oz drained canned bamboo
   shoots, sliced into thin batons
2 medium carrots, sliced into batons
130g/4½oz/1½ cups beansprouts
1 small white cabbage, shredded
30ml/2 tbsp Thai fish sauce
30ml/2 tbsp soy sauce
30ml/2 tbsp plum sauce
5ml/1 tsp sesame oil
15ml/1 tbsp palm sugar or light
   muscovado (brown) sugar
juice of ½ lime
90g/3½oz mooli (daikon), sliced into
   thin batons
small bunch fresh coriander
   (cilantro), chopped
30ml/2 tbsp sesame seeds, toasted

1 Cook the noodles in a large pan of boiling water, following the instructions on the packet. Meanwhile, heat the oil in a wok or large frying pan and stir-fry the ginger and garlic for 2–3 minutes over a medium heat, until golden.

2 Drain the noodles and set them aside. Add the bamboo shoots to the wok, increase the heat to high and stir-fry for 5 minutes. Add the carrots, beansprouts and cabbage and stir-fry for a further 5 minutes, until they are beginning to char on the edges.

3 Stir in the sauces, sesame oil, sugar and lime juice. Add the mooli and coriander, toss to mix, then spoon into a warmed bowl, sprinkle with toasted sesame seeds and serve immediately.

COOK'S TIP
Use a large, sharp knife for shredding cabbage. Remove any tough outer leaves, if necessary, then cut the cabbage into quarters. Cut off and discard the hard core from each quarter, place flat side down, then slice the cabbage very thinly to make fine shreds.

Energy 207kcal/866kJ; Protein 5.6g; Carbohydrate 42.3g, of which sugars 14.2g; Fat 1.6g, of which saturates 0.2g, of which polyunsaturates 0.6g; Cholesterol 0mg; Calcium 94mg; Fibre 4.1g; Sodium 682mg.

NOODLES AND VEGETABLES IN COCONUT SAUCE ★

WHEN EVERYDAY VEGETABLES ARE GIVEN THE THAI TREATMENT, THE RESULT IS A DELECTABLE DISH WHICH EVERYONE WILL ENJOY. NOODLES ADD BULK AND A WELCOME CONTRAST IN TEXTURE.

3 Increase the heat to medium, stir in the coconut milk and vegetable stock and bring to the boil. Add the broccoli florets and the noodles, lower the heat and simmer gently for 20 minutes.

4 Meanwhile, make the garnish. Split the lemon grass stalks lengthways through the root. Gather the coriander into a small bouquet and lay it on a platter, following the curve of the rim.

5 Tuck the lemon grass halves into the coriander bouquet and add the chillies to resemble flowers.

6 Stir the fish sauce, soy sauce and chopped coriander into the noodle mixture. Spoon on to the platter, taking care not to disturb the herb bouquet, and serve immediately.

SERVES SIX

INGREDIENTS
  10ml/2 tsp sunflower oil
  1 lemon grass stalk, finely chopped
  15ml/1 tbsp Thai red curry paste
  1 onion, thickly sliced
  3 courgettes (zucchini), thickly sliced
  115g/4oz Savoy cabbage,
    thickly sliced
  2 carrots, thickly sliced
  150g/5oz broccoli, stem sliced and
    head separated into florets
  2 × 400ml/14fl oz cans reduced-fat
    coconut milk
  475ml/16fl oz/2 cups vegetable stock
  150g/5oz dried egg noodles
  15ml/1 tbsp Thai fish sauce
  30ml/2 tbsp soy sauce
  60ml/4 tbsp chopped fresh
    coriander (cilantro)
For the garnish
  2 lemon grass stalks
  1 bunch fresh coriander (cilantro)
  8–10 small fresh red chillies

1 Heat the oil in a large pan or wok. Add the lemon grass and red curry paste and stir-fry for 2–3 seconds. Add the onion and cook over a medium heat, stirring occasionally, for about 5–10 minutes, until the onion has softened but not browned.

2 Add the courgettes, cabbage, carrots and slices of broccoli stem. Using two spoons, toss the vegetables with the onion mixture. Reduce the heat to low and cook gently, stirring occasionally, for a further 5 minutes.

Energy 181kcal/766kJ; Protein 7.2g; Carbohydrate 30.4g, of which sugars 12.3g; Fat 4.3g, of which saturates 1.1g, of which polyunsaturates 1.3g; Cholesterol 8mg; Calcium 115mg; Fibre 3.6g; Sodium 559mg.

CURRIED RICE VERMICELLI ★

SIMPLE AND SPEEDILY PREPARED, THIS DELICIOUS AND LIGHTLY FLAVOURED RICE NOODLE DISH WITH VEGETABLES AND PRAWNS IS ALMOST A COMPLETE MEAL IN A BOWL.

SERVES FOUR

INGREDIENTS

225g/8oz/2 cups dried rice vermicelli
10ml/2 tsp sunflower oil
1 egg, lightly beaten
2 garlic cloves, finely chopped
1 large fresh red or green chilli,
  seeded and finely chopped
15ml/1 tbsp medium curry powder
1 red (bell) pepper, thinly sliced
1 green (bell) pepper, thinly sliced
1 carrot, cut into matchsticks
1.5ml/¼ tsp salt
60ml/4 tbsp vegetable stock
115g/4oz cooked peeled prawns
  (shrimp), thawed if frozen
75g/3oz lean ham, cut into cubes
15ml/1 tbsp light soy sauce

1 Soak the rice vermicelli in a bowl of boiling water for 4 minutes, or according to the instructions on the packet, then drain thoroughly through a sieve or colander and set aside. Cover the bowl with a damp cloth or with clear film (plastic wrap) so that the vermicelli does not dry out.

2 Heat 5ml/1 tsp of the oil in a non-stick frying pan or wok. Add the egg and scramble until set, stirring with a pair of wooden chopsticks. Remove the egg with a slotted spoon and set aside.

3 Heat the remaining oil in the clean pan. Stir-fry the garlic and chilli for a few seconds, then stir in the curry powder. Cook for 1 minute, stirring, then stir in the peppers, carrot sticks, salt and stock.

4 Bring the mixture to the boil. Add the prawns, ham, scrambled egg, rice vermicelli and soy sauce. Mix well. Cook, stirring, until all the liquid has been absorbed and the mixture is hot. Serve immediately.

Energy 306kcal/1281kJ; Protein 16g; Carbohydrate 50.9g, of which sugars 6.5g; Fat 4.3g, of which saturates 0.9g, of which polyunsaturates 1.4g; Cholesterol 115mg; Calcium 56mg; Fibre 1.8g; Sodium 309mg.

MIXED MEAT NOODLES ★

A classic South-east Asian dish that originated in Singapore and has been adopted and adapted by its neighbouring countries. The noodles are standard street and café food, an ideal snack for anyone feeling a little peckish.

SERVES FOUR

INGREDIENTS

15ml/1 tbsp sesame oil
1 onion, finely chopped
3 garlic cloves, finely chopped
3–4 green or red Thai chillies,
    seeded and finely chopped
4cm/1½ in fresh root ginger,
    peeled and finely chopped
6 spring onions (scallions), chopped
1 skinless chicken breast fillet,
    cut into bitesize strips
90g/3½oz lean pork, cut into
    bitesize strips
90g/3½oz prawns (shrimp), shelled
2 tomatoes, skinned, seeded
    and chopped
30ml/2 tbsp tamarind paste
15ml/1 tbsp *nuoc mam*
grated rind and juice of 1 lime
10ml/2 tsp sugar
150ml/¼ pint/⅔ cup water or fish stock
225g/8oz fresh rice sticks (vermicelli)
salt and ground black pepper
1 bunch each fresh basil and mint,
    and *nuoc cham*, to serve

1 Heat a wok or heavy pan and add the sesame oil. Stir in the finely chopped onion, garlic, chillies and ginger, and cook until they begin to colour. Add the spring onions and cook for 1 minute, add the chicken and pork, and cook for 1–2 minutes, then stir in the prawns.

2 Add the tomatoes, followed by the tamarind paste, *nuoc mam*, lime rind and juice, and sugar to the pan and stir well. Pour in the water or fish stock, and stir again before cooking gently for 2–3 minutes. Bubble up the liquid to reduce it.

VARIATIONS
• At noodle stalls in street markets in Thailand and South-east Asia, batches of cold, cooked noodles are kept ready to add to whatever delicious concoction is cooking in the wok.
• At home, you can make this dish with any kind of noodles – egg or rice, fresh or dried.
• Cured Chinese sausage and snails, or strips of squid, are sometimes added to the mixture to ring the changes.

3 Meanwhile, toss the noodles in a large pan of boiling water and cook for a few minutes until tender.

4 Drain the noodles and add to the chicken and prawn mixture. Season with salt and ground black pepper.

5 Serve immediately, with basil and mint leaves sprinkled over the top, and drizzled with spoonfuls of *nuoc cham*.

COOK'S TIP
It's important to serve this dish immediately once the noodles have been added, otherwise they will go soft.

Energy 314kcal/1316kJ; Protein 19.2g; Carbohydrate 50.3g, of which sugars 5.9g; Fat 4g, of which saturates 0.6g, of which polyunsaturates 1.5g; Cholesterol 70mg; Calcium 74mg; Fibre 1.6g; Sodium 81mg.

WHEAT NOODLES WITH STIR-FRIED PORK ★★

THIS DELICIOUS RECIPE IS SIMPLICITY ITSELF WITH A WONDERFUL CONTRAST OF TEXTURES AND TASTE. THE PORK IS MARINATED IN PEANUT OIL WHICH ADDS A MARVELLOUSLY NUTTY FLAVOUR.

SERVES FOUR

INGREDIENTS
225g/8oz pork loin, cut into thin strips
225g/8oz dried wheat noodles, soaked
  in lukewarm water for 20 minutes
15ml/1 tbsp sunflower oil
2 garlic cloves, finely chopped
2–3 spring onions (scallions),
  trimmed and cut into
  bitesize pieces
45ml/3 tbsp *kroeung*
15ml/1 tbsp *tuk trey*
30ml/2 tbsp unsalted roasted
  peanuts, finely chopped
chilli oil, for drizzling (optional)
For the marinade
30ml/2 tbsp *tuk trey*
30ml/2 tbsp soy sauce
15ml/1 tbsp peanut oil
10ml/2 tsp sugar

1 In a bowl, combine the *tuk trey,* soy sauce, peanut oil and sugar for the marinade, stirring constantly until all the sugar dissolves. Toss in the strips of pork, making sure they are well coated in the marinade. Put aside for 30 minutes.

2 Drain the wheat noodles. Bring a large pan of water to the boil. Drop in the noodles, untangling them with chopsticks, if necessary. Cook for 4–5 minutes, until tender. Allow the noodles to drain thoroughly, then divide them among individual serving bowls. Keep the noodles warm until the dish is ready to serve.

3 Meanwhile, heat a wok. Add the oil and stir-fry the garlic and spring onions, until fragrant. Add the pork, tossing it around the wok for 2 minutes. Stir in the *kroeung* and *tuk trey* for 2 minutes, adding a splash of water if the wok gets too dry, and tip the pork on top of the noodles. Sprinkle the peanuts over the top to serve.

VARIATION
Wheat noodles are especially popular in Cambodia. Sold dried, in straight bundles like sticks, they are versatile and robust. Noodles drying in the open air, hanging from bamboo poles, are common in the markets. This simple recipe comes from a noodle stall in Phnom Penh. It also tastes excellent when made with fresh egg noodles.

Energy 340kcal/1435kJ; Protein 19.6g; Carbohydrate 46g, of which sugars 4.4g; Fat 9.9g, of which saturates 1.4g, of which polyunsaturates 2.6g; Cholesterol 35mg; Calcium 23mg; Fibre 1.9g; Sodium 41mg.

RICE NOODLES <u>WITH</u> PORK ★★

ALTHOUGH RICE NOODLES HAVE LITTLE FLAVOUR THEMSELVES THEY HAVE THE MOST WONDERFUL
ABILITY TO TAKE ON THE FLAVOUR OF OTHER INGREDIENTS.

<u>SERVES SIX</u>

INGREDIENTS
    450g/1lb lean pork fillet
    225g/8oz dried rice noodles
    115g/4oz/1 cup broccoli florets
    1 red (bell) pepper, quartered
      and seeded
    30ml/2 tbsp sunflower oil
    2 garlic cloves, crushed
    10 spring onions (scallions), trimmed
      and cut into 5cm/2in slices
    1 lemon grass stalk, finely chopped
    1–2 fresh red chillies, seeded and
      finely chopped
    300ml/½ pint/1¼ cups reduced-fat
      coconut milk
    15ml/1 tbsp tomato purée (paste)
    3 kaffir lime leaves (optional)
For the marinade
    45ml/3 tbsp light soy sauce
    15ml/1 tbsp rice wine
    15ml/1 tbsp oil
    2.5cm/1in piece of fresh root ginger

1 Cut the pork into strips about 2.5cm/1in long and 1cm/½in wide. Mix all ingredients for the marinade in a bowl, add the pork, stir to coat and marinate together for 1 hour.

2 Spread out the rice noodles in a shallow dish, pour over hot water to cover and soak for 20 minutes until soft. Drain.

3 Blanch the broccoli in a small pan of boiling water for 2 minutes, then drain and refresh under cold water. Set aside.

4 Place the pepper pieces under a hot grill (broiler) for a few minutes until the skin blackens and blisters. Put in a plastic bag for about 10 minutes and then, when cool enough to handle, peel away the skin and slice the flesh thinly.

5 Drain the pork, reserving the marinade. Heat half the oil in a large frying pan. Stir-fry the pork, in batches if necessary, for 3–4 minutes until the meat is tender. Transfer to a plate and keep warm.

6 Add a little more oil to the pan if necessary and fry the garlic, spring onions, lemon grass and chillies over a low to medium heat for 2–3 minutes. Add the broccoli and pepper and stir-fry for a few minutes more.

7 Stir in the reserved marinade, coconut milk and tomato purée, with the kaffir lime leaves, if using. Simmer gently until the broccoli is nearly tender, then add the pork and noodles. Toss over the heat, for 3–4 minutes until the noodles are completely heated through.

Energy 307kcal/1281kJ; Protein 19.5g; Carbohydrate 35.7g, of which sugars 5g; Fat 9.1g, of which saturates 2.1g, of which polyunsaturates 4g; Cholesterol 47mg; Calcium 44mg; Fibre 1.2g; Sodium 116mg.

VEGETARIAN AND SIDE DISHES

The vegetarian dishes in this chapter will provide
a healthy basis for many meals. All the recipes
stay well within sensible fat limits, and the side
dishes will complement any main course dish.
Delicious, aromatic curries include Corn and
Cashew Nut Curry, and Aubergine and Sweet
Potato Stew with Coconut Milk.

AUBERGINE CURRY WITH COCONUT MILK ★

AUBERGINE CURRIES ARE POPULAR THROUGHOUT SOUTH-EAST ASIA, THE THAI VERSION BEING THE MOST FAMOUS. ALL ARE HOT AND AROMATIC, ENHANCED WITH REDUCED-FAT COCONUT MILK.

2 Stir in the coconut milk and stock, and add the aubergines and lime leaves.

3 Partially cover the pan and simmer over a gentle heat for about 25 minutes until the aubergines are tender. Stir in the basil and check the seasoning. Serve with jasmine rice and lime wedges.

SERVES FOUR

INGREDIENTS
    15ml/1 tbsp sunflower oil
    4 garlic cloves, crushed
    2 shallots, sliced
    2 dried chillies
    45ml/3 tbsp *kroeung*
    15ml/1 tbsp palm sugar
    300ml/½ pint/1¼ cups reduced-fat
        coconut milk
    550ml/18fl oz/2¼ cups vegetable stock
    4 aubergines (eggplants), trimmed
        and cut into bitesize pieces
    6 kaffir lime leaves
    1 bunch fresh basil, stalks removed
    jasmine rice and 2 limes, cut into
        quarters, to serve
    salt and ground black pepper

1 Heat the sunflower oil in a wok or heavy pan until sizzling. Stir in the crushed garlic cloves, sliced shallots and whole chillies and stir-fry for a few minutes until they begin to colour. Stir in the *kroeung* and palm sugar, and stir-fry until the mixture begins to darken.

Energy 80kcal/338kJ; Protein 1g; Carbohydrate 12.3g, of which sugars 11.9g; Fat 3.4g, of which saturates 0.6g, of which polyunsaturates 1.9g; Cholesterol 0mg; Calcium 47mg; Fibre 1.2g; Sodium 139mg.

CORN AND CASHEW NUT CURRY ★★

A SUBSTANTIAL CURRY, THIS COMBINES ALL THE ESSENTIAL FLAVOURS OF SOUTHERN THAILAND.
IT IS DELICIOUSLY AROMATIC, BUT THE FLAVOUR IS FAIRLY MILD.

SERVES FOUR

INGREDIENTS
5ml/1 tsp sunflower oil
4 shallots, chopped
50g/2oz/½ cup cashew nuts
5ml/1 tsp Thai vegetarian red
  curry paste
400g/14oz potatoes, peeled and cut
  into chunks
1 lemon grass stalk, fincly chopped
200g/7oz can chopped tomatoes
600ml/1 pint/2½ cups boiling water
200g/7oz/generous 1 cup drained
  canned whole kernel corn
4 celery sticks, sliced
2 kaffir lime leaves, rolled into
  cylinders and thinly sliced
15ml/1 tbsp tomato ketchup
15ml/1 tbsp light soy sauce
5ml/1 tsp palm sugar or light
  muscovado (brown) sugar
4 spring onions (scallions), sliced
small bunch fresh basil, chopped

1 Heat the oil in a large, heavy pan or wok. Add the shallots and stir-fry over a medium heat for 2–3 minutes, until softened. Add the cashew nuts and stir-fry for a few minutes until golden.

2 Stir in the red curry paste. Stir-fry for 1 minute, then add the potatoes, lemon grass, tomatoes and boiling water.

3 Bring back to the boil, then reduce the heat to low, cover and simmer gently for 15–20 minutes, or until the potatoes are tender.

4 Stir the corn, celery, lime leaves, tomato ketchup, soy sauce and sugar into the pan or wok. Simmer for a further 5 minutes, until heated through, then spoon into warmed serving bowls. Sprinkle with the sliced spring onions and basil and serve.

COOK'S TIP
Rolling the lime leaves into cylinders before slicing produces very fine strips – a technique known as cutting *en chiffonnade*. Remove the central rib from the leaves before cutting them.

Energy 246kcal/1037kJ; Protein 6.9g; Carbohydrate 38.3g, of which sugars 12.7g; Fat 8.3g, of which saturates 1.6g, of which polyunsaturates 2.1g; Cholesterol 0mg; Calcium 40mg; Fibre 3.5g; Sodium 535mg.

TOFU AND VEGETABLE THAI CURRY ★★

TRADITIONAL THAI INGREDIENTS — CHILLIES, GALANGAL, LEMON GRASS AND KAFFIR LIME LEAVES — GIVE THIS CURRY A WONDERFULLY FRAGRANT AROMA. THE TOFU NEEDS TO MARINATE FOR AT LEAST 2 HOURS, SO BEAR THIS IN MIND WHEN TIMING YOUR MEAL.

SERVES FOUR

INGREDIENTS

175g/6oz firm tofu
45ml/3 tbsp dark soy sauce
5ml/1 tsp sesame oil
5ml/1 tsp chilli sauce
2.5cm/1in piece fresh root ginger, peeled and finely grated
1 head broccoli, about 225g/8oz
½ head cauliflower, about 225g/8oz
15ml/1 tbsp sunflower oil
1 onion, sliced
200ml/7fl oz/scant 1 cup reduced-fat coconut milk
350ml/12fl oz/1½ cups water
1 red (bell) pepper, seeded and chopped
175g/6oz/generous 1 cup green beans, halved
115g/4oz/1½ cups shiitake or button (white) mushrooms, halved
shredded spring onions (scallions), to garnish
boiled jasmine rice or noodles, to serve

For the curry paste
2 fresh red or green chillies, seeded and chopped
1 lemon grass stalk, chopped
2.5cm/1in piece fresh galangal, chopped
2 kaffir lime leaves
10ml/2 tsp ground coriander
a few fresh coriander (cilantro) sprigs, including the stalks
45ml/3 tbsp water

1 Rinse and drain the tofu. Using a sharp knife, cut it into 2.5cm/1in cubes. Place the cubes in the base of an ovenproof dish in a single layer.

2 Mix together the soy sauce, sesame oil, chilli sauce and grated ginger in a jug (pitcher) and pour over the tofu. Toss gently to coat all the cubes evenly, cover with clear film (plastic wrap) and leave to marinate for at least 2 hours or overnight if possible, turning and basting the tofu occasionally.

3 Make the curry paste. Place the chillies, lemon grass, galangal, lime leaves, ground coriander and fresh coriander in a food processor and process until well blended. Add the water and process to a thick paste.

4 Preheat the oven to 190°C/375°F/ Gas 5. Cut the broccoli and cauliflower into small florets. Cut any stalks into thin slices.

5 Heat the sunflower oil in a frying pan and add the sliced onion. Cook over a low heat for about 8 minutes, until soft and lightly browned. Stir in the curry paste and the coconut milk. Add the water and bring to the boil.

6 Stir in the red pepper, green beans, broccoli and cauliflower. Transfer to a Chinese sand pot or earthenware casserole. Cover and place towards the bottom of the oven.

7 Stir the tofu and marinade, then place the dish on a shelf near the top of the oven. Cook for 30 minutes. Remove both the dish and the sand pot or casserole from the oven. Add the tofu, with any remaining marinade, to the curry, with the mushrooms, and stir well.

8 Return the sand pot or casserole to the oven, reduce the temperature to 180°C/350°F/Gas 4 and cook for about 15 minutes, or until the vegetables are tender. Garnish with the spring onions and serve with the rice or noodles.

COOK'S TIP
Tofu or beancurd is made from soya beans and is sold in blocks. It is a creamy white colour and naturally low in fat. Tofu has a bland flavour and its absorbent nature means that it takes on the flavours of marinades or other foods with which it is cooked.

Energy 155kcal/646kJ; Protein 10.9g; Carbohydrate 12.2g, of which sugars 10.5g; Fat 7.2g, of which saturates 1.1g, of which polyunsaturates 3.8g; Cholesterol 0mg; Calcium 333mg; Fibre 5.3g; Sodium 875mg.

THAI VEGETABLE CURRY WITH LEMON GRASS RICE ★

FRAGRANT JASMINE RICE, SUBTLY FLAVOURED WITH LEMON GRASS AND CARDAMOM, IS THE PERFECT ACCOMPANIMENT FOR THIS RICHLY SPICED VEGETABLE CURRY.

SERVES FOUR

INGREDIENTS

    10ml/2 tsp sunflower oil
    200ml/7fl oz/scant 1 cup reduced-fat
      coconut milk
    550ml/18fl oz/2½ cups
      vegetable stock
    225g/8oz new potatoes, halved or
      quartered, if large
    8 baby corn cobs
    5ml/1 tsp golden caster
      (superfine) sugar
    185g/6½oz/1¼ cups broccoli florets
    1 red (bell) pepper, seeded and
      sliced lengthways
    115g/4oz spinach, tough stalks
      removed, leaves shredded
    30ml/2 tbsp chopped fresh
      coriander (cilantro)
    salt and ground black pepper
For the spice paste
    1 fresh red chilli, seeded
      and chopped
    3 fresh green chillies, seeded
      and chopped
    1 lemon grass stalk, outer leaves
      removed and lower 5cm/2in
      finely chopped
    2 shallots, chopped
    finely grated rind of 1 lime
    2 garlic cloves, chopped
    5ml/1 tsp ground coriander
    2.5ml/½ tsp ground cumin
    1cm/½in piece fresh galangal,
      finely chopped, or 2.5ml/½ tsp
      dried galangal (optional)
    30ml/2 tbsp chopped fresh
      coriander (cilantro)
    15ml/1 tbsp chopped fresh
      coriander (cilantro) roots and
      stems (optional)
For the rice
    225g/8oz/1¼ cups jasmine
      rice, rinsed
    6 cardamom pods, bruised
    1 lemon grass stalk, outer leaves
      removed, cut into 3 pieces
    475ml/16fl oz/2 cups water

1 Make the spice paste. Place all the ingredients in a food processor and process to a coarse paste. Heat the oil in a large, heavy pan. Add the paste and stir-fry over a medium heat for 1–2 minutes, until fragrant.

2 Pour in the coconut milk and stock and bring to the boil. Reduce the heat, add the potatoes and simmer gently for about 15 minutes, until almost tender.

3 Meanwhile, put the rice into a large pan with the cardamoms and lemon grass. Pour in the water. Bring to the boil, reduce the heat, cover, and cook for 10–15 minutes, until the water has been absorbed and the rice is tender.

4 When the rice is cooked and slightly sticky, season to taste with salt, then replace the lid and leave to stand for about 10 minutes.

5 Add the baby corn to the potatoes, season with salt and pepper to taste, then cook for 2 minutes. Stir in the sugar, broccoli and red pepper, and cook for 2 minutes more, or until the vegetables are tender.

6 Stir the shredded spinach and half the fresh coriander into the vegetable mixture. Cook for 2 minutes, then spoon the curry into a warmed serving dish.

7 Remove and discard the cardamom pods and lemon grass from the rice and fluff up the grains with a fork. Garnish the curry with the remaining fresh coriander and serve with the rice.

COOK'S TIP
Cardamom pods may be dark brown, cream, or pale green. The brown pods are usually larger, coarser and do not have such a good flavour as the others. Always remove them before serving.

Energy 313kcal/1313kJ; Protein 9.8g; Carbohydrate 61.4g, of which sugars 7.7g; Fat 3.2g, of which saturates 0.5g, of which polyunsaturates 1.5g; Cholesterol 0mg; Calcium 134mg; Fibre 4.1g; Sodium 439mg.

VEGETABLE FOREST CURRY ★

THIS IS A THIN, SOUPY CURRY WITH LOTS OF FRESH GREEN VEGETABLES AND ROBUST FLAVOURS. IN THE FORESTED REGIONS OF THAILAND, WHERE IT ORIGINATED, IT WOULD BE MADE USING EDIBLE WILD LEAVES AND ROOTS. SERVE IT WITH RICE OR NOODLES FOR A SIMPLE LUNCH OR SUPPER.

SERVES TWO

INGREDIENTS

   600ml/1 pint/2½ cups water
   5ml/1 tsp Thai vegetarian red
    curry paste
   5cm/2in piece fresh galangal or fresh
    root ginger
   90g/3½oz/scant 1 cup green beans
   2 kaffir lime leaves, torn
   8 baby corn cobs, halved widthways
   2 heads Chinese broccoli, chopped
   90g/3½oz/generous
    3 cups beansprouts
   15ml/1 tbsp drained bottled green
    peppercorns, crushed
   10ml/2 tsp granulated sugar
   5ml/1 tsp salt

1 Heat the water in a large pan. Add the red curry paste and stir until it has dissolved completely. Bring to the boil.

2 Meanwhile, using a sharp knife, peel and finely chop the fresh galangal or root ginger.

3 Add the galangal or ginger, green beans, lime leaves, baby corn cobs, broccoli and beansprouts to the pan. Stir in the crushed peppercorns, sugar and salt. Bring back to the boil, then reduce the heat to low and simmer for 2 minutes. Serve immediately.

Energy 154kcal/643kJ; Protein 14.9g; Carbohydrate 14.1g, of which sugars 11.8g; Fat 4.5g, of which saturates 0.8g, of which polyunsaturates 2.4g; Cholesterol 0mg; Calcium 173mg; Fibre 9.1g; Sodium 678mg.

JUNGLE CURRY ★

VARIATIONS OF THIS FIERY, FLAVOURSOME VEGETARIAN CURRY CAN BE FOUND ALL OVER SOUTHERN VIETNAM. A FAVOURITE WITH THE BUDDHIST MONKS AND OFTEN SOLD FROM COUNTRYSIDE STALLS, IT CAN BE SERVED WITH PLAIN RICE OR NOODLES, OR CHUNKS OF CRUSTY BREAD.

SERVES FOUR

INGREDIENTS

    15ml/1 tbsp sunflower oil
    2 onions, roughly chopped
    2 lemon grass stalks, roughly
       chopped and bruised
    4 green Thai chillies, seeded and
       finely sliced
    4cm/1½ in galangal or fresh root
       ginger, peeled and chopped
    3 carrots, peeled, halved lengthways
       and sliced
    115g/4oz yard-long beans
    grated rind of 1 lime
    10ml/2 tsp soy sauce
    15ml/1 tbsp rice vinegar
    5ml/1 tsp black peppercorns,
       crushed
    15ml/1 tbsp sugar
    10ml/2 tsp ground turmeric
    115g/4oz canned bamboo shoots
    75g/3oz spinach, steamed and
       roughly chopped
    150ml/¼ pint/⅔ cup reduced-fat
       coconut milk
    salt
    chopped fresh coriander (cilantro)
       and mint leaves, to garnish

COOK'S TIPS

• Yard-long beans are also known as asparagus beans or snake beans, and are eaten all over South-east Asia. They may grow up to 40cm/16in long and can be found in Asian stores. There are two common varieties, pale green and darker green, the latter having the better flavour. When buying, choose young, narrow specimens with under-developed seeds, as these will be the most tender. They do not have strings, and preparation is simply trimming and chopping them into short lengths. As they mature, snake beans can become quite tough. They should be used before they turn yellow.

• Jungle curry should be fiery, almost dominated by the chilli. In Vietnam it is often eaten for breakfast or a great pick-me-up at any time of day.

1 Heat a wok or heavy pan and add the oil. Once hot, stir in the onions, lemon grass, chillies and galangal or ginger. Add the carrots and beans with the lime rind and stir-fry for 1–2 minutes.

2 Add the soy sauce and rice vinegar to the wok and stir well. Add the crushed peppercorns, sugar and turmeric, then stir in the bamboo shoots and the chopped spinach.

3 Stir in the coconut milk and simmer for about 10 minutes, until the vegetables are tender. Season with salt, and serve hot, garnished with fresh coriander and mint.

Energy 119kcal/496kJ; Protein 3.8g; Carbohydrate 18.6g, of which sugars 15.3g; Fat 3.8g, of which saturates 0.5g, of which polyunsaturates 2.2g; Cholesterol 0mg; Calcium 125mg; Fibre 4.3g; Sodium 60mg.

AUBERGINE AND SWEET POTATO STEW
WITH COCONUT MILK ★

SCENTED WITH FRAGRANT LEMON GRASS, GINGER AND LOTS OF GARLIC, THIS IS A PARTICULARLY GOOD COMBINATION OF FLAVOURS. AUBERGINES AND SWEET POTATOES GO WELL TOGETHER AND THE COCONUT MILK ADDS A MELLOW NOTE.

SERVES SIX

INGREDIENTS

　400g/14oz baby aubergines
　　(eggplant) or 2 standard aubergines
　15ml/1 tbsp sunflower oil
　225g/8oz Thai red shallots or other
　　small shallots or pickling onions
　5ml/1 tsp fennel seeds,
　　lightly crushed
　4–5 garlic cloves, thinly sliced
　25ml/1½ tbsp finely chopped fresh
　　root ginger
　475ml/16fl oz/2 cups vegetable stock
　2 lemon grass stalks, outer layers
　　discarded, finely chopped
　　or minced
　15g/½oz/⅔ cup fresh coriander
　　(cilantro), stalks and leaves
　　chopped separately
　3 kaffir lime leaves, lightly bruised
　2–3 small fresh red chillies
　45ml/3 tbsp Thai green curry paste
　675g/1½ lb sweet potatoes, peeled
　　and cut into thick chunks
　400ml/14fl oz/1⅔ cups reduced-fat
　　coconut milk
　2.5–5ml/½–1 tsp palm sugar
　250g/9oz/3½ cups mushrooms,
　　thickly sliced
　juice of 1 lime, to taste
　salt and ground black pepper
　boiled rice and 18 fresh Thai basil
　　or ordinary basil leaves, to serve

1 Trim the aubergines. Slice baby aubergines in half lengthways. Cut standard aubergines into chunks.

2 Heat half the oil in a wide pan or deep, lidded frying pan. Add the aubergines and cook (uncovered) over a medium heat, stirring occasionally, until lightly browned on all sides. Remove from the pan and set aside.

3 Slice 4–5 of the shallots. Cook the whole shallots in the oil remaining in the pan, until lightly browned. Set aside with the aubergines. Add the remaining oil to the pan and cook the sliced shallots, fennel seeds, garlic and ginger over a low heat for 5 minutes.

4 Pour in the vegetable stock, then add the lemon grass, chopped coriander stalks and any roots, lime leaves and whole chillies. Cover and simmer over a low heat for 5 minutes.

5 Stir in 30ml/2 tbsp of the curry paste and the sweet potatoes. Simmer gently for about 10 minutes, then return the aubergines and browned shallots to the pan and cook for a further 5 minutes.

6 Stir in the coconut milk and the sugar. Season to taste with salt and pepper, then stir in the mushrooms and simmer gently for 5 minutes, or until all the vegetables are cooked and tender.

7 Stir in the remaining curry paste and lime juice to taste, followed by the chopped coriander leaves. Adjust the seasoning and ladle the vegetables into warmed bowls. Sprinkle basil leaves over the stew and serve with rice.

COOK'S TIP
Although this is called a stew, green curry paste is an important ingredient, as it is in most of these recipes. The quantity given is only a guide, however, so use less if you prefer.

Energy 147kcal/627kJ; Protein 3.2g; Carbohydrate 29.1g, of which sugars 11.3g; Fat 3g, of which saturates 0.6g, of which polyunsaturates 1.5g; Cholesterol 0mg; Calcium 72mg; Fibre 4.9g; Sodium 125mg.

GREEN MANGO SALAD ★

ALTHOUGH THE ORANGE AND YELLOW MANGOES AND PAPAYAS ARE DEVOURED IN VAST QUANTITIES, THEY ARE ALSO POPULAR WHEN GREEN. THEIR CRUNCHY TEXTURE MAKE THEM IDEAL FOR SALADS.

SERVES FOUR

INGREDIENTS

    450g/1lb green mangoes
    grated rind and juice of 2 limes
    30ml/2 tbsp sugar
    30ml/2 tbsp *nuoc mam*
    2 green Thai chillies, seeded and
      finely sliced
    1 small bunch fresh coriander
      (cilantro), stalks removed,
      finely chopped
    salt

1 Peel, halve and stone (pit) the green mangoes, and slice them into thin strips.

2 In a bowl, mix together the lime rind and juice, sugar and *nuoc mam*. Add the mango strips with the chillies and coriander. Add salt to taste and leave to stand for 20 minutes to allow the flavours to mingle before serving.

Energy 69kcal/293kJ; Protein 1.2g; Carbohydrate 16.2g, of which sugars 15.8g; Fat 0.4g, of which saturates 0.1g, of which polyunsaturates 0g; Cholesterol 0mg; Calcium 39mg; Fibre 3.6g; Sodium 7mg.

THAI ASPARAGUS ★

THIS IS AN EXCITINGLY DIFFERENT WAY OF COOKING ASPARAGUS. THE CRUNCHY TEXTURE IS RETAINED AND THE FLAVOUR IS COMPLEMENTED BY THE ADDITION OF GALANGAL AND CHILLI.

SERVES FOUR

INGREDIENTS

  350g/12oz asparagus stalks
  15ml/1 tbsp sunflower oil
  1 garlic clove, crushed
  15ml/1 tbsp sesame seeds, toasted
  2.5cm/1in piece fresh galangal,
    finely shredded
  1 fresh red chilli, seeded and
    finely chopped
  15ml/1 tbsp Thai fish sauce
  15ml/1 tbsp light soy sauce
  45ml/3 tbsp water
  5ml/1 tsp palm sugar or light
    muscovado (brown) sugar

VARIATIONS

Try this with broccoli or pak choi (bok choy). The sauce also works very well with green beans.

1 Snap the asparagus stalks. They will break naturally at the junction between the woody base and the more tender portion of the stalk. Discard the woody parts of the stems.

2 Heat the oil in a wok and stir-fry the garlic, sesame seeds and galangal for 3–4 seconds, until the garlic is just beginning to turn golden.

3 Add the asparagus stalks and chilli, toss to mix, then add the fish sauce, soy sauce, water and sugar. Using two spoons, toss over the heat for a further 2 minutes, or until the asparagus just begins to soften and the liquid is reduced by half.

4 Carefully transfer to a warmed platter and serve immediately.

Energy 50kcal/207kJ; Protein 3.4g; Carbohydrate 3.1g, of which sugars 3g; Fat 2.7g, of which saturates 0.4g, of which polyunsaturates 1.1g; Cholesterol 0mg; Calcium 50mg; Fibre 1.8g; Sodium 269mg.

PAK CHOI <u>WITH</u> LIME DRESSING ★

THE COCONUT DRESSING FOR THIS THAI SPECIALITY IS TRADITIONALLY MADE USING FISH SAUCE, BUT VEGETARIANS COULD USE MUSHROOM SAUCE INSTEAD. BEWARE, THIS IS A FIERY DISH!

SERVES FOUR

INGREDIENTS
- 15ml/1 tbsp sunflower oil
- 3 fresh red chillies, thinly sliced
- 4 garlic cloves, thinly sliced
- 6 spring onions (scallions), sliced diagonally
- 2 pak choi (bok choy), shredded
- 15ml/1 tbsp crushed peanuts

For the dressing
- 30ml/2 tbsp fresh lime juice
- 15–30ml/1–2 tbsp Thai fish sauce
- 250ml/8fl oz/1 cup reduced-fat coconut milk

1 Make the dressing. Put the lime juice and fish sauce in a bowl and mix well together, then gradually whisk in the coconut milk until combined.

2 Heat the oil in a wok and stir-fry the chillies for 2–3 minutes, until crisp. Transfer to a plate using a slotted spoon. Add the garlic to the wok and stir-fry for 30–60 seconds, until golden brown. Transfer to the plate.

3 Stir-fry the white parts of the spring onions for about 2–3 minutes, then add the green parts and stir-fry for 1 minute more. Transfer to the plate.

4 Bring a large pan of lightly salted water to the boil and add the pak choi. Stir twice, then drain immediately.

5 Place the pak choi in a large bowl, add the dressing and toss to mix. Spoon into a large serving bowl and sprinkle with the crushed peanuts and the stir-fried chilli mixture. Serve warm or cold.

VARIATION
If you don't like particularly spicy food, substitute red (bell) pepper strips for some or all of the chillies.

Energy 58kcal/244kJ; Protein 2.2g; Carbohydrate 5g, of which sugars 4.8g; Fat 3.5g, of which saturates 0.5g, of which polyunsaturates 2g; Cholesterol 0mg; Calcium 113mg; Fibre 1.4g; Sodium 408mg.

THAI-STYLE YAM ★

THE FOOD OF SOUTHERN THAILAND IS NOTORIOUSLY HOT, AND THIS DELIGHTFULLY TANGY FLAVOURED DISH MAKES THE PERFECT ACCOMPANIMENT TO ANY SPICY MEAL.

SERVES FOUR

INGREDIENTS

- 90g/3½ oz Chinese leaves (Chinese cabbage), shredded
- 90g/3½ oz/generous 1 cup beansprouts
- 90g/3½ oz/scant 1 cup green beans, trimmed
- 90g/3½ oz broccoli, preferably the purple sprouting variety, divided into florets
- 15ml/1 tbsp sesame seeds, toasted

For the yam

- 120ml/4fl oz/½ cup reduced-fat coconut milk
- 5ml/1 tsp Thai red curry paste
- 90g/3½ oz/1¼ cups oyster mushrooms or field (portabello) mushrooms, sliced
- 5ml/1 tsp ground turmeric
- 5ml/1 tsp thick tamarind juice, made by mixing tamarind paste with warm water
- juice of ½ lemon
- 60ml/4 tbsp light soy sauce
- 5ml/1 tsp palm sugar or light muscovado (brown) sugar

1 Steam the shredded Chinese leaves, beansprouts, green beans and broccoli separately or blanch them in boiling water for 1 minute per batch. Drain, place in a serving bowl and leave to cool.

2 Make the yam. Pour half the coconut milk into a wok and heat gently for 2–3 minutes, until it separates. Stir in the red curry paste. Cook over a low heat for 30 seconds, until the mixture is fragrant.

3 Increase the heat to high and add the mushrooms to the wok or pan. Cook for a further 2–3 minutes.

4 Pour in the remaining coconut milk and add the ground turmeric, tamarind juice, lemon juice, soy sauce and sugar to the wok or pan. Mix thoroughly.

5 Pour the mixture over the prepared vegetables and toss well to combine. Sprinkle with the toasted sesame seeds and serve immediately.

COOK'S TIP
Oyster mushrooms need gentle handling. Tear large specimens apart and don't overcook them or they will be rubbery.

Energy 68kcal/286kJ; Protein 4g; Carbohydrate 7g, of which sugars 6.1g; Fat 2.9g, of which saturates 0.5g, of which polyunsaturates 1.3g; Cholesterol 0mg; Calcium 75mg; Fibre 2.4g; Sodium 1108mg.

DESSERTS

Thai and South-east Asian desserts fit perfectly into a healthy diet. Very often, these desserts consist of a huge platter of fresh fruits intended to refresh and cleanse the palate after a spicy meal. Ices and jellies are popular too, especially when based on fruit or coconut.

WATERMELON ICE ★

AFTER A HOT AND SPICY THAI MEAL, THE ONLY THING MORE REFRESHING THAN ICE-COLD WATERMELON IS THIS WATERMELON ICE. MAKING IT IS SIMPLICITY ITSELF.

3 Spoon the watermelon into a food processor. Process to a slush, then mix with the sugar syrup. Chill the mixture in the refrigerator for 3–4 hours.

4 Strain the mixture into a freezerproof container. Freeze for 2 hours, then remove from the freezer and beat with a fork to break up the ice crystals. Return the mixture to the freezer and freeze for 3 hours more, beating the mixture at half-hourly intervals. Freeze until firm.

5 Alternatively, use an ice-cream maker. Pour the chilled mixture into the machine and churn until it is firm enough to scoop. Serve immediately, or scrape into a freezerproof container and store in the freezer.

6 About 30 minutes before serving, transfer the ice to the refrigerator so that it softens slightly. This allows the full flavour of the watermelon to be enjoyed and makes it easier to scoop.

SERVES FOUR TO SIX

INGREDIENTS
   90ml/6 tbsp caster
     (superfine) sugar
   105ml/7 tbsp water
   4 kaffir lime leaves, torn into
     small pieces
   500g/1¼lb watermelon

1 Put the sugar, water and lime leaves in a pan. Heat gently until the sugar has dissolved. Pour into a large bowl and set aside to cool.

2 Cut the watermelon into wedges with a large knife. Cut the flesh from the rind, remove the seeds and chop.

Energy 62kcal/263kJ; Protein 0.1g; Carbohydrate 16.3g, of which sugars 16.3g; Fat 0g, of which saturates 0g, of which polyunsaturates 0g; Cholesterol 0mg; Calcium 9mg; Fibre 0g; Sodium 1mg.

COCONUT SORBET ★★

DELICIOUSLY REFRESHING AND COOLING, THIS SORBET CAN BE FOUND IN DIFFERENT VERSIONS ALL OVER SOUTH-EAST ASIA. OTHER CLASSIC SORBETS ARE MADE WITH LYCHEES AND PINEAPPLE.

SERVES SIX

INGREDIENTS

175g/6oz/scant 1 cup caster (superfine) sugar
120ml/4fl oz/½ cup reduced-fat coconut milk
50g/2oz/⅔ cup grated or desiccated (dry unsweetened shredded) coconut
a squeeze of lime juice

1 Place the sugar in a heavy pan and add 200ml/7fl oz/scant 1 cup water. Bring to the boil, stirring constantly, until the sugar has dissolved completely. Reduce the heat and simmer for 5 minutes to make a light syrup.

2 Stir the coconut milk into the sugar syrup, along with most of the coconut and the lime juice. Pour the mixture into a bowl or freezer container and freeze for 1 hour.

3 Take the sorbet out of the freezer and beat it with a fork, or blend it in a food processor, until it is smooth and creamy, then return it to the freezer and leave for 30 minutes.

4 Remove the sorbet from the freezer again and beat it with a fork, or blend it in a food processor, until it is smooth and creamy. Then return it to the freezer and leave until completely frozen.

5 Before serving, allow the sorbet to stand at room temperature for 10–15 minutes to soften slightly. Serve in small bowls and decorate with the remaining grated coconut.

COOK'S TIP
This refreshing sorbet is very welcome on a hot day, or as a palate refresher during a spicy meal. You could serve it in coconut shells, garnished with sprigs of fresh mint.

Energy 170kcal/717kJ; Protein 0.7g; Carbohydrate 32g, of which sugars 32g; Fat 5.2g, of which saturates 4.5g, of which polyunsaturates 0.1g; Cholesterol 0mg; Calcium 23mg; Fibre 1.1g; Sodium 26mg.

COCONUT JELLY WITH STAR ANISE FRUITS ★

SERVE THIS DESSERT AFTER ANY ASIAN-STYLE MEAL WITH PLENTY OF REFRESHING EXOTIC FRUIT.
THE COMBINATION OF REDUCED-FAT COCONUT MILK WITH FRESH STAR FRUIT AND LYCHEES MAKES
FOR A DELICIOUS AND SURPRISINGLY REFRESHING LOW-FAT DESSERT.

SERVES FOUR

INGREDIENTS
250ml/8fl oz/1 cup cold water
75g/3oz/⅓ cup caster (superfine)
sugar
15ml/1 tbsp powdered gelatine
400ml/14fl oz/1⅔ cups reduced-fat
coconut milk
For the syrup and fruit
250ml/8fl oz/1 cup water
3 star anise
50g/2oz/¼ cup caster (superfine) sugar
1 star fruit, sliced
12 lychees, peeled and stoned (pitted)
115g/4oz/1 cup blackberries

1 Pour the water into a pan and add the sugar. Heat gently until the sugar has dissolved. Sprinkle over the gelatine and heat gently, stirring, until the gelatine has dissolved. Stir in the coconut milk, remove from the heat and set aside.

2 Grease an 18cm/7in square tin (pan). Line with clear film (plastic wrap). Pour in the milk mixture and chill until set.

3 To make the syrup, combine the water, star anise and sugar in a pan. Bring to the boil, stirring, then lower the heat and simmer for 10–12 minutes until syrupy. Place the fruit in a heatproof bowl and pour over the hot syrup. Cool, then chill.

4 To serve, cut the coconut jelly into diamonds and remove from the tin. Arrange the coconut jelly on individual plates, adding a few of the fruits and their syrup to each portion.

COOK'S TIP
Coconut milk is available in cans or cartons. It has a high fat content so look out for the reduced-fat version which can be up to 88 per cent fat free.

Energy 246kcal/1051kJ; Protein 4.4g; Carbohydrate 60g, of which sugars 60g; Fat 0.4g, of which saturates 0.2g, of which polyunsaturates 0.1g; Cholesterol 0mg; Calcium 67mg; Fibre 1.5g; Sodium 114mg.

JUNGLE FRUITS IN LEMON GRASS SYRUP ★

THIS EXOTIC AND REFRESHING FRUIT SALAD CAN BE MADE WITH ANY COMBINATION OF TROPICAL FRUITS — JUST GO FOR A GOOD BALANCE OF COLOUR, FLAVOUR AND TEXTURE. YOU CAN ALSO FLAVOUR THE SYRUP WITH GINGER RATHER THAN LEMON GRASS, IF YOU PREFER.

SERVES SIX

INGREDIENTS
- 1 firm papaya
- 1 small pineapple
- 2 small star fruit, sliced into stars
- 12 fresh lychees, peeled and stoned (pitted) or 14oz/400g can lychees
- 2 firm yellow or green bananas, peeled and cut diagonally into slices
- mint leaves, to decorate

For the syrup
- 115g/4oz/generous ½ cup caster (superfine) sugar
- 2 lemon grass stalks, bruised and halved lengthways

1 To make the syrup, put 225ml/ 7½ fl oz/1 cup water into a heavy pan with the sugar and lemon grass stalks. Bring to the boil, stirring constantly until the sugar has dissolved, then reduce the heat and simmer for 15 minutes. Leave to cool.

2 Peel and halve the papaya, remove the seeds and slice the flesh crossways. Peel the pineapple and slice it into rounds. Remove the core and cut each round in half. (Keep the core and slice it for a stir-fry.)

3 Put all the fruit into a bowl. Pour the syrup, including the lemon grass stalks, over the top and toss to combine. Cover and chill for 6 hours, or overnight. Before serving, remove the lemon grass stalks and decorate with mint leaves.

Energy 174kcal/742kJ; Protein 1.3g; Carbohydrate 44.2g, of which sugars 43.4g; Fat 0.3g, of which saturates 0g, of which polyunsaturates 0.1g; Cholesterol 0mg; Calcium 38mg; Fibre 2.7g; Sodium 6mg.

STEWED PUMPKIN IN COCONUT CREAM ★

FRUIT STEWED IN COCONUT MILK IS A POPULAR DESSERT IN THAILAND. PUMPKINS, BANANAS AND MELONS CAN ALL BE PREPARED IN THIS SIMPLE BUT TASTY WAY.

SERVES FOUR TO SIX

INGREDIENTS
  1kg/2¼ lb kabocha pumpkin
  750ml/1¼ pints/3 cups reduced-fat
    coconut milk
  175g/6oz/¾ cup granulated sugar
  pinch of salt
  4–6 fresh mint sprigs, to decorate

COOK'S TIP
To make the decoration, wash the pumpkin seeds to remove any fibres, then pat them dry on kitchen paper. Roast them in a dry frying pan, or spread them out on a baking sheet and grill (broil) until golden brown, tossing them frequently to prevent them from burning.

1 Cut the pumpkin in half using a large, sharp knife, then cut away and discard the skin. Scoop out the seed cluster. Reserve a few seeds and throw away the rest. Using a sharp knife, cut the pumpkin flesh into pieces that are about 5cm/2in long and 2cm/¾in thick.

2 Pour the coconut milk into a pan. Add the sugar and salt and bring to the boil. Add the pumpkin and simmer for about 10–15 minutes, until it is tender. Serve warm, in individual dishes. Decorate each serving with a mint sprig and toasted pumpkin seeds (see Cook's Tip).

MANGOES WITH STICKY RICE ★

STICKY RICE IS JUST AS GOOD IN DESSERTS AS IN SAVOURY DISHES, AND RIPE MANGOES, WITH THEIR DELICATE FRAGRANCE AND VELVETY FLESH, COMPLEMENT IT ESPECIALLY WELL.

SERVES FOUR

INGREDIENTS
  115g/4oz/⅔ cup white
    glutinous rice
  175ml/6fl oz/¾ cup reduced-fat
    coconut milk
  45ml/3 tbsp granulated sugar
  pinch of salt
  2 ripe mangoes
  strips of pared lime rind,
    to decorate

1 Rinse the glutinous rice thoroughly in several changes of cold water, then leave to soak overnight in a bowl of fresh cold water.

COOK'S TIP
Like dairy cream, the thickest and richest part of coconut milk always rises to the top. Whenever you open a can or carton, spoon off this top layer and use the thinner, lower fat bottom layer in cooking.

2 Drain the rice well and spread it out evenly in a steamer lined with muslin or cheesecloth. Cover and steam over a pan of simmering water for about 20 minutes, or until the rice is tender.

3 Reserve 45ml/3 tbsp of the cream from the top of the coconut milk. Pour the remainder into a pan and add the sugar and salt. Heat, stirring constantly, until the sugar has dissolved, then bring to the boil. Remove the pan from the heat, pour the coconut milk into a bowl and leave to cool.

4 Tip the cooked rice into a bowl and pour over the cooled coconut milk mixture. Stir well, then leave the rice mixture to stand for 10–15 minutes.

5 Meanwhile, peel the mangoes, cut the flesh away from the central stones (pits) and cut into slices.

6 Spoon the rice on to individual serving plates. Arrange the mango slices on one side, then drizzle with the reserved coconut cream. Decorate with strips of lime rind and serve.

Top: Energy 164kcal/701kJ; Protein 1.7g; Carbohydrate 40.3g, of which sugars 39.4g; Fat 0.7g, of which saturates 0.4g, of which polyunsaturates 0g; Cholesterol 0mg; Calcium 100mg; Fibre 1.7g; Sodium 139mg.
Bottom: Energy 200kcal/846kJ; Protein 3.1g; Carbohydrate 46g, of which sugars 24.3g; Fat 0.8g, of which saturates 0.2g, of which polyunsaturates 0g; Cholesterol 0mg; Calcium 32mg; Fibre 2g; Sodium 51mg.

PUMPKIN PUDDING IN BANANA LEAVES ★

THIS IS A TRADITIONAL PUDDING THAT CAN BE MADE WITH SMALL, SWEET PUMPKINS, OR BUTTERNUT SQUASH WITH DELICIOUS RESULTS. THIS TASTY DESSERT CAN BE EATEN HOT OR COLD.

2 In a pan, heat the coconut milk with the sugar and a pinch of salt. Blend the tapioca starch with 15ml/1 tbsp water and 15ml/1 tbsp of the hot coconut milk. Add it to the coconut milk and beat well. Beat the mashed pumpkin into the coconut milk or, if using a blender, add the coconut milk to the pumpkin and purée together.

3 Spoon equal amounts of the pumpkin purée into the centre of each banana leaf square. Fold in the sides and thread a cocktail stick (toothpick) through the open ends to enclose the purée.

4 Fill the bottom third of a wok with water. Place a bamboo steamer on top. Place as many stuffed banana leaves as you can into the steamer, folded side up – you may have to cook them in batches. Cover the steamer and steam parcels for 15 minutes. Unwrap them and serve hot or cold.

SERVES SIX

INGREDIENTS
    1 small pumpkin, about 1.3kg/3lb,
      peeled, seeded and cubed
    250ml/8fl oz/1 cup reduced-fat
      coconut milk
    45ml/3 tbsp palm sugar
    15ml/1 tbsp tapioca starch
    12 banana leaves, cut into 15cm/6in
      squares

VARIATION
You can also try sweet potatoes, cassava or taro root in this recipe.

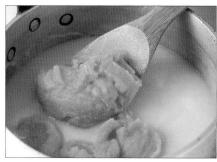

1 Bring a pan of salted water to the boil. Add the pumpkin flesh and cook for 15 minutes, or until tender. Drain and mash with a fork or purée in a blender.

STEAMED CUSTARD IN NECTARINES ★

STEAMING NECTARINES OR PEACHES BRINGS OUT THEIR NATURAL COLOUR AND SWEETNESS, SO THIS IS A GOOD WAY OF MAKING THE MOST OF UNDERRIPE OR LESS FLAVOURFUL FRUIT.

SERVES SIX

INGREDIENTS
6 nectarines
1 large (US extra large) egg
45ml/3 tbsp light
muscovado (brown) sugar
or palm sugar
30ml/2 tbsp reduced-fat
coconut milk

COOK'S TIP
Palm sugar, also known as jaggery, is made from the sap of certain Asian palm trees, such as coconut and palmyrah. It is available from Asian food stores. If you buy it as a cake or large lump, grate it before use.

1 Cut the nectarines in half. Using a teaspoon, scoop out the stones (pits) and a little of the surrounding flesh.

2 Lightly beat the egg, then add the sugar and the coconut milk. Beat until the sugar has dissolved.

3 Transfer the nectarines to a steamer and carefully fill the cavities three-quarters full with the custard mixture. Steam over a pan of simmering water for 5–10 minutes. Remove from the heat and leave to cool completely before transferring to plates and serving.

Energy 119kcal/507kJ; Protein 3.8g; Carbohydrate 25.2g, of which sugars 25.2g; Fat 1.1g, of which saturates 0.3g, of which polyunsaturates 0.1g; Cholesterol 32mg; Calcium 24mg; Fibre 2.3g; Sodium 20mg.

TAPIOCA WITH BANANA AND COCONUT ★

POPULAR IN BOTH VIETNAM AND CAMBODIA, THIS IS THE TYPE OF DESSERT THAT EVERYBODY'S MOTHER OR GRANDMOTHER MAKES. SWEET AND NOURISHING, IT IS MADE WITH TAPIOCA PEARLS COOKED IN COCONUT MILK AND SWEETENED WITH BANANAS AND SUGAR.

SERVES FOUR

INGREDIENTS
550ml/18fl oz/2½ cups water
40g/1½oz tapioca pearls
550ml/18fl oz/2½ cups reduced-fat
  coconut milk
90g/3½oz/½ cup sugar
3 ripe bananas, diced
salt

COOK'S TIP
A pinch of salt added to this recipe enhances the flavour of the coconut milk and counterbalances the sweetness. You can try the recipe with sweet potato, taro root, yellow corn or rice.

1 Pour the water into a pan and bring it to the boil. Stir in the tapioca pearls, reduce the heat and simmer for about 20 minutes, until translucent. Add the coconut milk, sugar and a pinch of salt. Cook gently for 30 minutes.

2 Stir the diced bananas into the tapioca and coconut milk mixture and cook for 5–10 minutes until the bananas are soft but not mushy. Spoon into individual warmed bowls and serve immediately.

Energy 226kcal/964kJ; Protein 1.5g; Carbohydrate 57.2g, of which sugars 45.9g; Fat 0.7g, of which saturates 0.4g, of which polyunsaturates 0.1g; Cholesterol 0mg; Calcium 57mg; Fibre 0.9g; Sodium 154mg.

BAKED RICE PUDDING, THAI-STYLE ★

BLACK GLUTINOUS RICE, ALSO KNOWN AS BLACK STICKY RICE, HAS LONG DARK GRAINS AND A NUTTY TASTE REMINISCENT OF WILD RICE. THIS BAKED PUDDING HAS A DISTINCT CHARACTER AND FLAVOUR ALL OF ITS OWN, AS WELL AS AN INTRIGUING APPEARANCE.

SERVES SIX

INGREDIENTS
　175g/6oz/1 cup white or black
　　glutinous rice
　30ml/2 tbsp soft light brown sugar
　475ml/16fl oz/2 cups reduced-fat
　　coconut milk
　250ml/8fl oz/1 cup water
　3 eggs
　30ml/2 tbsp granulated sugar

1 Combine the glutinous rice and brown sugar in a pan. Pour in half the coconut milk and the water.

2 Bring to the boil, reduce the heat to low and simmer, stirring occasionally, for 15–20 minutes, or until the rice has absorbed most of the liquid. Preheat the oven to 150°C/300°F/Gas 2.

3 Spoon the mixture into a large ovenproof dish or individual ramekins. Beat the eggs with the remaining coconut milk and sugar in a bowl.

4 Strain the egg mixture into a jug (pitcher), then pour it evenly over the par-cooked rice in the dish or ramekins.

5 Place the dish or ramekins in a roasting pan. Carefully pour in enough hot water to come halfway up the sides of the dish or ramekins.

6 Cover with foil and bake for about 35–60 minutes, or until the custard has set. Serve warm or cold.

COOK'S TIP
Throughout South-east Asia, black glutinous rice is usually used for sweet dishes, while its white counterpart is more often used in savoury recipes.

Energy 198kcal/834kJ; Protein 5.9g; Carbohydrate 36.2g, of which sugars 14.3g; Fat 3.5g, of which saturates 0.9g, of which polyunsaturates 0.3g; Cholesterol 95mg; Calcium 47mg; Fibre 0g; Sodium 124mg.

INDEX